Juvenile Procedures in California

8TH Edition

by

Edward E. Peoples, DPA
Professor Emeritus
Administration of Justice Department
Santa Rosa Junior College

Distributed by

Meadow Crest Publishing
Forestville, CA 95436
Phone or Fax (707) 887-1877.
e-mail: Meadowcrestpublishing@msn.com

Copyright © 2019 by Edward E. Peoples

ISBN# 978-0-9985884-1-4

All rights reserved. No part of this book may be reproduced, stored in a retrieval system, transcribed, or transmitted in any form for any purpose without the prior written permission of the author.
Please respect the rights of the author

This book is dedicated to the Memory of
William E. Thornton
Former Chief Probation Officer
County of Sacramento
For his wisdom, insight, humor and friendship
And for his contribution to juvenile law and reform

Brief Table of Contents

Preface

Chapter 1	The Evolution of Juvenile Justice	1
Chapter 2	The Status Offender, Pre-1976`	13
Chapter 3	Current Status Offender Procedures	22
Chapter 4	Police Procedures with Law Violators	36
Chapter 5	Special Law Enforcement Procedures	52
Chapter 6	Juvenile Due Process and Jurisdictional Waiver Procedures	80
Chapter 7	Pre-Court Procedures	96
Chapter 8	Juvenile Court Proceedings	109
Chapter 9	Probation Services	126
Chapter 10	The Division of Juvenile Facilities	142
Chapter 11	The Dependent Child - Physical and Emotional Abuse	155
Chapter 12	Child Sexual Abuse and Dependency Court Proceedings	176
Case Index		201
Subject Index		203

PREFACE

Juveniles are handled differently by the agents and agencies of government than are adults. These differences are expressed primarily in three ways:

- the goals of the juvenile system have an unique nature and purpose

- a distinct body of law exists to direct juvenile procedures and those who would implement them

- an unique legal vocabulary exists to describe the procedures and to reflect the goals

Given these distinctions, it follows that a specific body of knowledge exists to be learned by those who will work within the system or who have need to understand its operation.

To date, few current texts are available that focus just on juvenile procedures. Most texts are very broad in scope and emphasize the theoretical aspects of delinquency so as to appeal to the widest audience. This leaves the instructors and the students the burden of translating the broad theories and concepts into a legal and procedural framework as they apply within the state.

The aim of this work is to narrow the scope of presentation, and to limit the applications, in order to aid in that translation. The material that follows is intended for use in California college and university courses that focus on juvenile law and procedures. It may also be used in law enforcement or probation academy classes, as a supplemental text.

The intent herein is to provide scholarly, current, and well-researched material, presented in a very direct, basic, and readable style. This 8th edition contains updates in case law and procedures to the previous edition and presents the same basic content in a logical sequence. This edition is primarily an update to include content and case decisions, and to update procedures for the state's institutional and parole components, where significant changes have occurred. The presentation begins in Chapter I with a look at the historical influences that have shaped our system.

Chapter 2 examines one category of juveniles that come within the system, status offenders, as they were handled before 1976. Status offenders are juveniles, whose behavior is illegal only because of their age status, i.e., disobeying parents and teachers, running away from home, truanting, or leading a *wayward life*.

Chapter 3 details the current procedures that apply in status offender situations, with the inclusion of curfew and loitering laws. Chapter 4 details the procedures that police must and/or may follow in dealing with juveniles suspected of law violations. It includes both the statutory and case law that provides the legal guidance for police in taking a minor into temporary custody, and detaining a minor in a law enforcement facility.

Chapter 5 focuses on special procedures for police in three areas: the guarantees of the Fifth and Sixth Amendments for juveniles; school searches, and the searches of probationers and parolees; and street gang laws and suppression techniques.

Chapter 6 reviews five major U.S. Supreme Court decisions and their impact on juvenile law, rights, and procedures when the appellate court extended certain constitutional guarantees to juvenile proceedings. Following this, the chapter examines certain procedures that were created by the passage of Proposition 21 on March 8, 2000, mandating and/or allowing adult prosecution of qualifying minors. In this chapter, details the recent change in **Juvenile Court Law by SB 1391**, signed into law on August 30, 2018, that prohibits juveniles ages 15 and under from being tried as adult. This modified Section 707 of the Welfare & Institutions Code, and represents a significant change in how crimes by juveniles under the age of sixteen years are treated.

Chapter 7 presents the procedures that apply in the pre-court stages of juvenile proceedings. This begins with the initial intake of a juvenile into the court and probation systems, after a minor has been referred by law enforcement. The roles of a probation intake officer and the district attorney are detailed, as are the alternatives to formal court proceedings.

The complete formal juvenile court proceedings are presented in Chapter 8, along with the procedure that is used as the alternative to the formal court process, known as deferred entry of judgment. The various dispositions that the court imposes on juveniles are reviewed as well.

Chapter 9 focuses on the nature, scope, and purposes of probation, including the roles of, and services provided by, county probation officers.

In 2005, state corrections, both for adults and juveniles, were reorganized into one umbrella agency, the California Department of Corrections and Rehabilitation (CDCR). Under that umbrella, the Division of Juvenile Justice (DJJ) was created, and under that sub-organization is the Division of Juvenile Facilities (DJF), the new name of the agency that administers the state-run system of juvenile institutions.

This agency, DJF, was known for many years as the California Youth Authority (CYA), and that title will undoubtedly be slow to leave the lexicon of juvenile procedures. However, since 2014, the state component of juvenile justice has been either closed or incorporated into the adult system. Parole has become the supervision responsibility of county probation departments, upon the release of wards from an institution.

Also, under DJJ is the Division of Parole Operations, was responsible to administer juvenile parole services. This is not the actual parole board, but merely handles the services and parole supervision for juveniles released on parole. The various parole boards were reorganized in 2005, and both adult and juvenile parole boards were blended into one board, the Board of Parole Hearings. The procedures that have evolved out of these divisions are the subject of Chapter 10.

Child abuse is covered in the concluding two chapters. Chapter 11 details the nature and scope of child abuse and neglect, with a focus on physical assault and physical and emotional neglect. This includes the responsibilities of law enforcement and Child Protective Services. Child sexual abuse and exploitation are covered in Chapter 12, along with dependency proceedings in juvenile court. Aftercare procedures for dependent cases are examined in this chapter as well.

A list of key terms and concepts is included at the beginning of each chapter as a study guide for the student. References and a complete list of all appellate case decisions are provided at the end of each chapter for those seeking to pursue research in any of the areas studied.

The term *police* is used often throughout this book when describing certain procedures of the juvenile justice system. Within this context, the use of the word *police* is meant as a generic term referring to any and all law enforcement, including local police, deputy sheriffs, CHP or state police, and other appropriate policing agents or agencies. They are all engaged in the same task of regulating and controlling human behavior within the limits of the law.

Table of Contents

Chapter 1   The Evolution of Juvenile Justice
Key Terms and Concepts   1
    Introduction   1
    Age of Responsibility   2
    The English Experience   3
    The American Experience   5
    Reform Begins   7
    The California System   8
    A Reform School System Develops   9
    Juvenile Court and Probation Services   10
    A Revolution in Juvenile Court Law   11
    Summary   11
    References   12
    Case Decisions   12

Chapter 2   The Status Offender, Pre-1976
    Key Terms and Concepts   13
    Introduction   13
    The Status Offender, Pre-1976   14
    How the System Created Delinquents   16
    A Legal Challenge to the System   17
    The Traditional Approach Continued   18
    The Seeds of Revolution   19
    Summary   20
References   21
Internet References   21
Case Decisions   21

Chapter 3   Current Status Offender Procedures
Key Terms and Concepts   22
Introduction   22
The Revolution of 1976   22
The Current Section 601   23
Impact of the Dixon Bill   24
Community Resources for 601s   25
Recent Modifications in 601 Procedures   25
    Missing Person Procedures   26
    601 Truancy Procedures   28

        Police Searches of Truants   30
        601 Curfew/Loitering Procedures   31
        The Case of In re Daniel D., 1995   32
Summary   33
References   34
Internet References   34
Case Decisions   35

Chapter 4   Police Procedures with Law Violators

    Key Terms and Concepts   36
    Introduction   36
    Functional Specialization   36
    The Beat Officer   37
    Delinquency: A Legal Definition   37
    Police-Juvenile Transactions   38
        Consensual Encounter   38
        Detention   39
        Police Authority to Arrest   40
Police Options After Taking Custody of Minors   41
Police Interrogation of Juveniles   45
Minor's Right to Make Phone Calls   45
Voluntary Chemical testing of Minors   45
Custody of Minors in Law Enforcement Facilities   46
    Secure Detention in a Locked Room   47
    Non-secure Detention   48
Regulations for Any Minors Detained   48
    Summary   50
    References   50
Internet references   50
    Case Decisions   51

Chapter 5   Special Law Enforcement Procedures

    Key Terms and Concepts   52
    Introduction   52
    Fifth and Sixth Amendment Protections   52
        The Miranda Requirement   53
    California Law   56
    Miranda in Federal Juvenile Cases   58
    Interested Adult Laws   59
    Fourth Amendment Protection   60

        The Exclusionary Rule   60
        School Searches   61
        Police Searches of Probationers   64
        Parole Searches   66
Juvenile Gangs: Control and Suppression   67
    Gang Formations and Activities   68
    Why Juveniles Join Gangs   69
    California's Legal Definition of a Street Gang   69
    Punishment for Street Gang Offenses   70
    Street Gang Registration Requirements   71
    Police Gang Suppression   72
Task or Strike Force Organizations   73
Summary   73
References   74
Case Decisions   75

Chapter 6   Juvenile Due Process and Jurisdictional Waiver Procedures
Key Terms and Concepts   76
    Introduction   76
    Juvenile Due Process Cases   77
        Kent v. U. S., 1966   77
    In re Gault, 1967   79
    In re Winship, 1970   80
    McKeiver v. Pennsylvania, 1971   81
Breed v. Jones, 1975   82
Jurisdiction Waiver Procedures   83
        Senate Bill 1391   85
        Section 707 WIC   86
        The Judicial Waiver   90
        The Transfer (Fitness) Hearing   91
        Criteria for Transfer (Fitness)   92
        Judicial Finding of Fitness   91
    Alternative Waiver Procedures   92
    Summary   93
    References   94
    Case Decisions   95

Chapter 7   Pre-Court Procedures
Key Terms and Concepts   96
    Introduction   96
    Probation: Organization and Functions   97

        The Role of Probation Intake   97
        The Discretion of Intake   101
        The Discretion of the District Attorney   102
Steps Toward Adjudication   102
        The Petition   102
        The Detention Hearing   104
        The Criteria for Detention   105
Detention: The Juvenile Hall   106
        Establishing a Prima Facie Case   107
Summary   107
Internet References   108
Case Decisions   108s

Chapter 8   Juvenile Court Proceedings

Key Terms and Concepts   109
Introduction   109
The Adjudication/Jurisdictional Hearing   109
        The Hearing Process   110
        Defense Strategies   111
        The Finding   112
        Admission of the Public   113
The Dispositional Process   113
        Purpose of Juvenile Court Law   114
        Punishment Does Not Include Retribution   115
        The Probation Officer's Report   115
        The Dispositional Hearing   116
        Informal Probation   117
        Wardship   118
        Out-of-Home Placement   119
        County Camp, Ranch, or School Commitment   119
        Commitment to the State Division of Juvenile Facilities   120
Deferred Entry of Judgment   119
The Citation Hearing   122
Supplemental Petition Procedures   123
Summary   124
Case Decisions   125

Chapter 9   Probation Services

Key Terms and Concepts   126
Introduction   126

      Organization of Probation Services   126
      Functional Specialization   127
Authority of a Probation Officer   128
      Probation Intake   128
      Court Investigation   129
      Supervision of Probation Cases   129
      Caseload Size and Assignment Models   131
      Regular Supervision   132
      Conditions of Probation   132
Juvenile Re-Entry Grants: the New Role for
                            Juvenile Court and Probation   134
Inter and Intra-State Transfer Cases   136
Termination of Wardship and Probation   136
Sealing of Records   137
Violations and Revocation of Probation   138
Summary   140
Case Decisions   140

Chapter 10   The Division of Juvenile Facilities
      Key Terms and Concepts   142
      Introduction   142
      Brief History of the Division of Juvenile Facilities   143
DJF's Population Profile   and Cost   145
DJF Programs   145
The Juvenile Parole Board   146
The Purposes of a DJF Commitment   148
The DJF Commitment: Calculating the Commitment Time   148
The Board's Authority   146
The DJF Commitment: The Board Confinement Time   1150
Programming and Review   150
      Discharge (Parole) Consideration   151
      Division of Parole Operations   152
Summary   153
Internet References   153
      Case Decisions   154

Chapter 11   The Dependent Child: Physical and Emotional Abuse
      Key Terms and Concepts   155
      The Dependent Child and Police Authority   157
      Dependent Child: §300 WIC   157
Law Enforcement Authority   157

Police Discretion and Alternative Dispositions 160
The Categories of Child Abuse 163
Physical Assault 163
    Criminal Law Violations 164
    Who Are the Abusers? 164
    Police Intervention 165
    Indicators of Abuse 167
Police Questioning and Discretion 168
Physical Neglect 170
The Law Enforcement Investigation 171
Emotional Maltreatment 172
Emotional Assault 172
Consequences of Emotional Assault 173
Indicators of Assault 173
Emotional Deprivation 173
Indicators of Deprivation 174
Consequences of Deprivation 174
Summary 174
References 175
Internet References 175

Chapter 12 Child Sexual Abuse and Dependency Court Proceedings

Key Terms and Concepts 176
Introduction 176
Sexual Abuse 177
    Sexual Abuse Defined 177
    Sexual Assault 177
    Sexual Exploitation 178
The Dynamics of Sexual Abuse and Exploitation 179
The Sex Offender 181
Intra-familial Abuse 181
Extra-familial Abuse 182
Sexual Exploitation and Pornography 183
Police Intervention 184
Indicators of Sexual Abuse and Exploitation 186
Consequence of Abuse and Exploitation 186
Child Protective Services 188
Child Abuse Reporting Laws 190
Sex Offender Registration 191
Juvenile Court Dependency Proceedings 192

    Basis for Dependency 193
    The Role of Intake 193
    The Petition 194
    The Detention Hearing 195
    The Adjudication/Jurisdictional Hearing 196
    The Dispositional Hearing 197
  Summary 198
  References 199
  Internet References 200
  Case Decisions 200

Case Index 201

Subject Index 203

Chapter 1: The Evolution of Juvenile Justice

Key terms and Concepts

Age of responsibility	Juvenile Court Law of 1961
Ah Peens	King's Chamberlain's Court
Borstel system	*Loco parentis*
Chancery court	*Parens patriae*
Civil proceedings	Petition
Delinquent	Poor Laws of 1600s
Dependent, abused child	Preponderance of evidence
House of Refuge	Status offender
Illinois Juvenile court Act, 1899	

Introduction

California's juvenile justice system evolved out of our English common law heritage. However, special codes for juveniles existed in most every culture long before the English experience.

These early laws regulated what might be considered criminal conduct, such as theft or burglary, but they also controlled a juvenile's social conduct and his or her relationships with adults. They stressed obedience, education, hard work, respect for elders, and a good moral life. Thus, certain laws controlling the behavior of some individuals mere because of their age status were present quite early in our history. These types of laws came to be called **status offenses**.

Punishments for law violations were severe and were designed to correct the child for his or her *own good*; and juveniles had no rights as individuals. They did what adults told them to do and had no protection from abuse. Our laws have evolved over the years and today juveniles have almost all the rights of an adult, and they receive far more protections than adults.

The Age of Responsibility

The juvenile system was erected upon three conceptual pillars. The first and foremost of these is the **age of responsibility**. That is, at what age is a person responsible for his or her conduct? The answer is, it all depends. It all depends on what the offense is and in what state the juvenile commits the offense. States vary on their legal definition of adulthood for purposes of criminal prosecution. Usually it is between ages 16 to 18 years and older.

Twenty-three states now have no lower age limit at which an individual may face criminal prosecution. In 1999, an 11-year-old Michigan boy became the youngest person in modern American history to be prosecuted in criminal court. In November 2000, a 13-year-old Philadelphia girl was prosecuted as an adult for a murder she allegedly committed in August 1999, when she was 11 years old.

Many states have a minimum age under which an individual is considered too young to even enter the juvenile justice system. North Carolina uses a minimum age of six. Maryland, Massachusetts and New York use age 7 as the minimum. Arizona and California use the minimum age of 8 years. Arkansas, Colorado, Kansas, Louisiana, Minnesota, Mississippi, Pennsylvania, South Dakota, Texas, Vermont, and Wisconsin use the minimum age of 10 years.

All states have provisions by which a juvenile may be found unfit to remain within the juvenile system and may be transferred to adult court to stand criminal trial. Between 1992 and 1997, 47 states enacted laws making the process easier to try juveniles as adults.

California lowered the age from 16 to 14 years for certain offenses during the 1994 session of the Legislature, effective January 2, 1995. More recently, California voters approved **Proposition 21**, known as the **Gang Violence and Juvenile Crime Prevention Act of 1998**, at the polls on March 7, 2000, that substantially changed the nature of juvenile procedures for minors age 14 years or older, who are accused of committing certain listed felonies. This will be discussed in a later chapter.

The impact of these changes in California law will be discussed in the relevant portions of this text. Suffice it to say at this point that in California all persons under the age of 18 years shall be treated as juveniles unless specific provisions of the law require or allow otherwise, as described above.

The English Experience

Under English **common law** children ages seven and under were not responsible and not held accountable for their acts. They did not enter the system except as dependent or neglected children. Those individuals 14 and over were fully responsible and were treated like any other adult with corporal or capital punishment, or transportation to a penal colony. Youths between ages eight and thirteen who were accused of offenses were brought before the Court solely for the purpose of determining responsibility. The issue for the Court was whether a youth was capable of forming intent, whether he or she knew right from wrong, and could appreciate the consequences of his or her act. Those found responsible were punished as adults. Penal colony records show a number of boys and girls ages eight to thirteen who had been transported there to serve time.

Responsibility is a fundamental issue in deciding how to deal with today's youth. It is the basis for establishing and maintaining juvenile systems in each state. Every time legislation is enacted to treat juveniles differently than adults, the question must be addressed: at what age is a person responsible?

Two other concepts join that of responsibility, to form the trilogy upon which juvenile procedures are founded. One concept is ***parens patriae***, a Latin phrase, which translates to mean *the King is father of the country*. This implies the responsibility of the State. Like any good father, the King is responsible for the welfare of his subjects, particularly those who cannot care for themselves.

The application of this concept emerged in 12th century England when the King's Chancery Court was created in London to hear *petitions* for aid and relief for those in need. These petitions were made primarily on behalf of children who had no one to provide for their support. These were the dependent and neglected children. Those under age 14 could be placed as apprentices under a master in some trade, or in homes to work as servants. Wherever they were placed, they were expected to be industrious and obedient. However, as one might expect, not all the children went along with the program. Some ran away and others disobeyed. Thus, the State (King), by trying to help one category of juveniles, the dependent, created a second category, the status offender - the runaway and the incorrigible.

A special court, the **King's Chamberlain's Court** (or City Custom of Apprentices) was created to deal with this new problem. Here, the second philosophical concept of *loco parentis* came into play. When translated, this Latin phrase means, "*to stand in place of the parent.*" This implies the authority of the King (State) to step in and become the legal parent. Now the State had both the responsibility to help and the authority to define the problem and the solution.

The Chamberlain's Court was the forerunner of our present day juvenile court. It was established under the protective umbrella of *parens patriae* and the benevolent authority of *loco parentis*. The hearings were private and confidential, and due process was never considered an issue. The purpose was to settle down the unruly child and to teach him or her the habits of industry, for his or her own good.

The use of these juvenile courts was increased during the late 1500s and early 1600s when a series of **Poor Laws** were enacted to help remove the increasing number of poor urchins roaming the streets of London. Many were begging, but many others were running in gangs and stealing. Their parents could not or would not control them.

These Poor Laws expanded the King's authority to intervene in the family and decide which juveniles needed removal and placement in apprenticeships or to work in private homes. The age of jurisdiction for the incorrigible or wayward child was extended to eighteen. Those who became incorrigible or runaways for a second time, or sometimes a third time, were treated as wayward delinquents and either were hanged, transported to a penal colony, or jailed in congregate cells at London's Newgate Prison. Records show that during the early 1800s, hundreds of young boys and girls were thrown together in prison with every type of adult criminal. You can imagine the range of inmate behaviors that greeted them there.

Thousands of children were placed in the stocks and whipped by their parents for misconduct. Many "stout and healthy boys" were committed to the Marine Society, an organization formed in 1756 by Jonas Hanway, a London philanthropist and Sir John Fielding, a London magistrate. In 1758 Fielding also sponsored a group home called the House of Refuge for Orphan Girls. By 1788 a private institution was funded by a London reformer, Robert Young, to house dependent and neglected children and status offenders. The purpose was "...to educate and instruct them in some useful trade or occupation."

Reform efforts grew during the 1800s and focused on separating juveniles from adult offenders and placing them in a facility where they could receive education, training, and treatment instead of punishment. By 1850 the Borstel (reform school) system was developed and commonly used in England.

The American Experience

Since America was British first we accepted the common law principles of *parens patriae* and *loco parentis* and the age of responsibility. Youths under age eight were incapable of forming intent, those fourteen and over were fully responsible for their actions, while those between eight and thirteen were given what could be called responsibility hearings. If a jury found an accused juvenile guilty and capable of "…discerning between good and evil…," the minor would receive an adult sentence, usually corporal or capital punishment.

Fortunately, delinquency was not as widespread in America as it was in England. Fortunately, too, for those juveniles found guilty of offenses, most were found *not responsible* by sympathetic juries. The so-called wayward children, those not receiving an education or occupational training under their parents' direction, were removed from their homes and placed with master craftsmen or indentured, as it were, as servants; boys until age eighteen and girls until age twenty-one.

By the early 1800s, some of the larger cities were experiencing a delinquency problem. In New York, a commission appointed to study the problem found that between 1817 and 1821 seventy-five youths per year were sent to adult jails, while most of those released as *not responsible*, continued in their delinquent ways. The Commission reported that:

> ➢ those juveniles who were locked up learned more and better ways to commit crimes
> ➢ those left unpunished were encouraged to re-offend

The Commission's Report recommended separate facilities for juveniles, and the recommendation was followed. In 1824 the city of New York opened its first **House of Refuge**. Boston followed in 1826 and Philadelphia in 1828. The purpose of the houses of refuge was **threefold**:
> ➢ to separate the juveniles from the adult offender

- to protect juveniles from evil influences
- to educate, train, and treat juveniles instead of punishing them

The intent of this reform was well meaning, but the softness in the wording was somehow lost in the application. Most juveniles experienced hard work, severe discipline, and brutal corporal punishment. It did not matter whether the child was in for stealing, running away from placement, or leading an immoral life. They were all treated alike.

This right of the court to remove a child from its parental home was challenged in Ohio in 1838, when a young girl, Mary Ann Crouse, was taken from her parents' custody and committed to a refuge for being a "wayward girl." The father filed a Writ of *Habeas Corpus* with the Ohio Supreme Court, claiming that his daughter was deprived of her freedom without due process. The Court ruled against the father and upheld the right of the State to become the substitute parent. Since the juvenile hearing followed civil procedures and the court was acting on behalf of the minor, not against her, it was legal and no constitutional due process rights were necessary. The court would provide all the protection needed.

By the mid-1800s the House of Refuge concept was adopted by most states and they were established as state reformatories. These seemed successful at first. However, during the 1870s and 1880s, the economy fell into a recession and it became increasingly difficult for states to adequately fund their institutional programs. Institutional managers had to develop alternative sources of funding. Many brought in industries on a contract basis: shoe, clothing, and shirt factories were established. Others used a contract indenture system in which juveniles were leased to households, or to shippers and whalers, or apprenticed in a trade. In many cases, the institution would send a representative out west to take orders from households, stores, and farms for juveniles to work at various jobs. Then, they would escort a trainload of boys and girls out west to fill these orders.

The original protective reform life was transformed into custody at hard work, and many social reformers were concerned that these schools had merely replaced one form of punishment with another equally as bad and legally unfair.

Reform Begins

Reformers pushed for other alternatives that were not as punitive. **John Augustus**, the so-called "father of probation," had used probation successfully in Boston since 1841. As he noted in his journal:

> I bailed nineteen boys, from 7 to 15 years of age, and in bailing them it was understood, and agreed by the court, that their cases should be continued from term to term for several months, as a season of probation; thus, each month at the calling of the docket, I would appear in court, make my report, and thus the cases would pass on for 5 or 6 months. At the expiration of this term, twelve of the boys were brought into court at one time, and the scene formed a striking and highly pleasing contrast with their appearance when first arraigned. The judge expressed much pleasure as well as surprise at their appearance, and remarked that the object of law had been accomplished and expressed his cordial approval of my plan to save and reform.

The efforts of Augustus over the next twenty years set the tone for the reformative approach that would follow. By 1890 the Pennsylvania Children's Aid Society received cooperation from the local court to place juveniles, under their supervision, in foster homes. The New York Society for the Prevention of Cruelty to Children followed suit, while Massachusetts expanded its welfare agencies to take on the same placement and supervision responsibilities.

The stage was set by the end of the century with all the principles, practices, and concepts ready to be codified into final form. In 1899 the **Illinois Juvenile Court Act** was passed, and it created the model used in most states today. A separate juvenile court was created in which proceedings were civil, confidential and without the due process necessary in criminal proceedings. A **preponderance of the evidence** (just over half) was sufficient for a finding of delinquency.

The common law principles of *parens patriae* and *loco parentis* were expressed in statutory law, along with the practices of filing a **petition** on behalf of a minor. The law also established separate detention and institutional facilities for juveniles, as well as a probation staff to provide supervision for the minor in his or her home.

The juvenile justice system as we know it today became a legal reality. This protective umbrella has been given an overlay of due process in recent years, forcing it to evolve into a system full of inconsistencies and self-canceling procedures, as we shall see in a later chapter. By 1910, 32 states had established juvenile courts and separate juvenile systems, including probation services. By 1925, all but two states had followed suit.

The California System

Delinquency was late in coming to California, as were social problems in general. Consequently, the development of a juvenile justice system came later than it did in the east. However, when it did emerge, it assumed the same nature that had been formed by British common law and the Illinois model. By the 1870s, juveniles up to age twenty-one accused of either criminal offenses or status offenses were tried as adults and, if convicted, were sentenced like adults. This often meant serving time in state prison. Between 1850 and 1860 some 300 boys were sent to San Quentin. This included some boys as young as 12 who were found *responsible*, and were committed for their *own good*. Boys were also committed to the San Francisco Industrial School.

In 1876, the appellate case of a young Chinese boy, Ah Peen, confirmed the concepts of *parens patriae* and *loco parentis* as the basis of juvenile proceedings in California. Ah Peen, a sixteen-year-old boy, had been found delinquent by a judge and committed to the San Francisco Industrial School for "...*leading an idle and dissolute life*." A relative appealed to the State Supreme Court claiming that Ah Peens had been deprived of his freedom without due process. The Court disagreed and held that:

> ...provisions of the Constitution have no application whatever to the case of this minor child. The action...here in question did not amount to a criminal prosecution....The purpose in view is not punishment for offenses done, but reformation and training of the child to habits of industry, with a view to his future usefulness when he shall have been reclaimed to society, or shall have attained his majority. Having been abandoned by his parents, the State as *parens patriae*, has succeeded to his control, and stands in *loco parentis* to him. The restraint imposed

upon him by public authority is in its nature and purpose the same which, under other conditions, is habitually imposed by parents, guardians of the person, and others exercising supervision and control over the conduct of those who are by reason of infancy, lunacy, or otherwise, incapable of properly controlling themselves.

Thus, the precedent was set. Juvenile proceedings were civil and any actions taken **on behalf of** the minor were legal. As we shall see below, very little has changed in how a delinquent is processed today; and up to the mid-1970s status offenders were still treated almost the same as they were in the time of Mary Ann Crouse and Ah Peen.

A Reform School System Develops
The San Francisco Industrial School was established by the Legislature on May 5, 1859, with a capacity for 48 boys and girls ages 13 to 18 years. In 1860 the State Reform School of Marysville opened but it was closed in 1868 because of low population. The 28 boys committed there were transferred to the San Francisco Industrial School, and the state agreed to pay $15 in gold coin per month for each child detained. In 1868 the girls in the San Francisco Industrial School were transferred to the Magdelen Asylum in San Francisco.

In 1875 the training ship *Jamestown* was transferred from the Navy to the City of San Francisco to supplement the Industrial School as a place of commitment for boys. They were given training in seamanship and navigation, and after six months were eligible for employment as seamen on merchant ships. Within four years, however, the ship was returned to the Navy due to mismanagement and complaints that the *Jamestown* was really a training ship for criminals.

The need for placement facilities for juveniles continued to grow, and most people wanted to have juveniles completely separated from adults. Finally, in 1890 the legislature enacted a law establishing a state reform school system, and by 1892 the San Francisco Industrial School was closed. The Whittier State Reformatory for Boys and Girls opened in 1891 with 300 youths, and Preston School of Industry (the *Castle*) opened to house the older boys in 1895. By 1907 all youths under age 18 were transferred from San Quentin to these reform schools. By 1913 girls were separated from boys and were transferred from Whittier to the new Ventura School.

Juvenile Court and Probation Services

The twentieth century brought with it the call for more reform, for an alternative for juveniles to the adult court system. The call was heard but not well supported at first. Finally, a separate juvenile court and juvenile probation system were created by the Legislature in 1903, but they were tacked on as an afterthought in the appendix of the Penal Code. The age of adulthood was set initially at 16, and then changed to age 18 in 1909.

The role of a probation officer was cast in an authoritarian mold under the control of the superior court in each county. It was left up to the local judges how to staff and administer probation services. A 1904 law authorized the State Board of Charities and Corrections to oversee the juvenile justice and probation system, but as that Board soon learned, each county court was a power unto itself.

In 1905 legislation required judges to appoint a probation committee to help select the probation officer. At the same time, the law was expanded to provide for county juvenile detention facilities, written probation court reports, and procedures for committing juveniles to the state reform schools at Whittier and Preston. Jurisdiction over all juvenile matters was given to the superior court of each county.

Confusion still existed over the exact procedures required for handling dependent and delinquent cases. Conflict existed, as well, between reform groups and local judges over the intent of the juvenile legislation. A compromise was achieved resulting in the Juvenile Court Law of 1915, detailing the procedures to follow in handling each category of juveniles, the essence of which prevailed until 1961. The juvenile justice system developed throughout California at a lagging pace, and as late as 1929, three counties still did not have probation officers. In addition, the over-riding concern for local control made standard procedures and practices impossible. Wide disparity existed from county to county over how juveniles were treated.

Reform efforts came and went to no avail for many years until Karl Holton, a California Youth Authority administrator, convinced Governor Goodwin Knight in 1957 to appoint a juvenile justice commission to study the problems. Governor Edmund Brown renewed the Commission's appointment when he took office the following year. Finally, a small dedicated group of reformers within the Commission, and within the justice system itself, neutralized the opposition and put together a new juvenile court law which Governor Brown included in his legislative proposal in 1961.

In September 1961, the new juvenile court law became operative, and revolutionized juvenile procedures in California.

A Revolution in Juvenile Court Law

The 1961 law was termed a revolution (Lemert, 1970) because, for the first time in California, standardized procedures were provided in a Welfare and Institutions Code (WIC) for law enforcement agencies, the courts, and probation departments to follow in handling juveniles. Descriptions of behavior by which the police and court could exercise jurisdiction over juveniles were narrowed, and specific distinctions were made between real delinquents (§602 WIC) and status offenders (§601WIC).

Dependent/neglected cases (originally §600 WIC and changed to §300 in 1976) also were re-defined and new procedures were implemented to protect abused minors. They could no longer be mixed or housed with the 601s or 602s in a juvenile hall. Court procedures were made more legalistic, and new roles and responsibilities were created for probation to standardize intake powers and procedures from county to county. Procedures also were included to reduce court commitments of status offenders to the Youth Authority. In short, much of our present-day juvenile justice system was codified in 1961.

Summary

Our juvenile justice system evolved primarily from English common law and was erected on three pillars: the age of responsibility, parens *patriae*, and *loco parentis*. Each state has established the age difference between an adult and a juvenile, usually ranging between 16 to 18 years, with provisions for referring certain juveniles to criminal court for trial as adults. The age for juveniles in California was set at under 18 years, with the noted exception that will be detailed in the relevant chapters to follow.

As the juvenile system evolved in California, the superior court of each county was responsible to establish and maintain a juvenile court and probation services; and local control was the rule.

It took many years, and the efforts of many reformers to move the system from the punitive days in refuges and reform schools to the Juvenile Court Law of 1961. The man to whom this text is dedicated, Warren E. Thornton, played a large role in formulating that law and those procedures. This revolutionized juvenile procedures by providing a Welfare and Institutions Code that codified the categories of delinquent (§602), status offender §601), and the dependent/neglected child (§600), and standardized many of the procedures for police, probation, and the courts.

A second revolution in juvenile court law occurred in 1976, when the legislature significantly altered how police, courts, and probation could deal with status offenders and, to a lesser degree, how delinquents could be treated. That law and the current procedures mandated by this 1976 legislation (the Dixon Bill) is the focus of the chapter to follow.

References

Augustus, John. *John Augustus, First Probation Officer: John Augustus' Original Report on this Labors - 1852.* Mountclair, N. J.: Patterson Smith, 1972.

Burdman, Milton; Winslow Rouse and Stuart Adams. *Probation in California.* Sacramento: California Board of Corrections, 1957.

Lemert, Edwin M. *Social Action and Legal Change: Revolution within the Juvenile Court.* Chicago: Aldine, 1970.

Case Decisions

Ex Parte (In re) Ah Peen (1876) 2 Cal. Rptr. 280
Ex Parte (In re) Crouse, (1838) 4 Whart. 1 Prescott v. Ohio, 19 Ohio 184

Chapter 2: The Status Offender: Pre-1976

Key Terms and Concepts

Allegation
Beyond control
Curfew
Escalating the offense
Family Systems Theory
Incorrigible
Labeling theory

Loitering
Medical model
Petition
Runaway
Status offense
Truancy
Void-for-vagueness doctrine
§601 WIC

Introduction

The incorrigible side of the nature of juveniles has been an irritant for adults ever since there have been children. According to William Shakespeare:

> *I would there were no age between sixteen and twenty-three, or that the Youth would sleep out the rest; for there is nothing in the between but Getting wenches with child, wronging the ancestry, stealing, fighting...*
>
> Act III, Scene III, *The Winter's Tale*

In most cultures this conduct typically expressed by minors has been regulated to help parents maintain control over their children. In California minors under the age of eighteen years are prohibited from disobeying their parents or teachers, running away from home, truanting from school, or violating curfew laws. These are called status offenses because they affect a group of people of a specific age status.

A **status offense**, then, is *any act prohibited by law for juveniles that is non-criminal*. The legal description of the conduct that brings a minor within the jurisdiction of the juvenile justice system is found in Section 601 of the Welfare and Institutions Code (WIC, or W & I Code):

The Status Offender, 1961-1976

The legal description given in §601 WIC, which was codified in 1961, stated:

> ➢ Any person under the age of 21 years who persistently or habitually refuses to obey the reasonable and proper orders or directions of his parents, guardian, custodian, or school authorities, or who is beyond the control of such person, or any person who is a habitual truant from school within the meaning of any law of this state, or who from any cause is in danger of leading an idle, dissolute, lewd or immoral life, is within the jurisdiction of the juvenile court which may adjudge such person to be a ward of the court.

Note that the age limit for a status offense was up to 21 years. Police intervention with incorrigible and runaway minors was frequent and parent could call police, complain that their child was beyond their control, and police would dispatch a patrol car to the home. If the parents desired police would take the minor into temporary custody (arrest) and deliver him or her to the local county juvenile hall. Reported runaways would be pursued actively by police and when found, also would be delivered to the juvenile hall.

Police often took minors into custody for conduct defined as "...*being in danger of leading an idle, dissolute, lewd or immoral life*...," either at the request of parents or on their own motion. This usually meant that the minor was found involved in some sort of sexual behavior, drinking, fighting, or loitering in the wrong place at the wrong hours.

It was used as a *catch-all* offense when police had no other legal way to take juveniles into custody. It was also used by probation departments in a similar manner or on occasions when they did not want to become involved in a situation referred to them. For example, this writer witnessed several incidents in juvenile hall in which the parents of a juvenile girl would come to a probation Intake Officer wanting charges of statutory rape (consensual sex) filed against their daughter's boyfriend.

Intake would agree, but would then state that charges of "…being in danger of leading an idle, dissolute, lewd or immoral life…" would be filed on behalf of their daughter in that she consented to the sexual relations. The parents usually would withdraw their allegations against the boyfriend, and everyone would go home, not very happy.

After booking any 601 in the juvenile hall by police the case would be referred to an on-duty probation officer working in the position called **Intake**. This officer was responsible for screening the case and deciding what action to take to resolve any problems. Theoretically, any action taken would be in the best interest of the minor. It would be done to protect the minor from others or from himself or herself. In fact, far too often the minor was blamed for the act and was held accountable to change, or face the consequences. The fact that the parents might be incompetent, unreasonable, or abusive was not often taken into consideration. The fact that a minor might be running away from a home in which he or she was physically or sexually abused was rarely an issue.

If the Intake Officer, parents, and child agreed that no agency action was necessary, the minor would be admonished (scolded) by Intake and the matter dismissed. If Intake or the parents thought that some agency support short of court action was necessary, the minor could be placed under six months informal probation. This meant that the final decision was delayed for six months during which the minor was supervised by a probation officer. It was the officer's responsibility to resolve any problems so that the minor would become obedient.

If the parents or Intake thought the minor's problems required more formal action, Intake would file a **§601petition** with the Court to declare the minor a ward. The **petition** is the legal document in which the **allegation** (charge) of runaway or being beyond control would be described. It is the legal request for the court to intervene as the benevolent parent (*parens patriae*), to take control (*loco parentis*) and provide the guidance necessary for the minor to grow into adulthood as a responsible person.

At this point, if the parents did not want the minor home, or if the minor would not return home, or if Intake thought the minor should not go home, the minor would be detained in juvenile hall pending court proceedings. The minor would be brought to court within 48 hours where a judge or court referee or commissioner would explain the petition to the minor and his or her parents, set a court date, and decide if further detention was necessary. If detained, the minor would be placed in a living unit within the juvenile hall by age or maturity, not by offense category. Consequently, status offenders were mixed with delinquents of all sorts. Juvenile hall staff treated runaways or incorrigibles the same as they would burglars, car thieves, or murderers.

The full details of the juvenile court process will be explained in the chapter on delinquents. Suffice it to say here that many status offenders were adjudged wards of the court and placed on probation. Conditions of probation usually included an order to obey the parents and school authorities, report to the probation officer as directed, attend school regularly, and not associate with selected peers. A curfew might be included as well.

How the System Created Delinquents

A **status offender ward** could be returned home on probation, placed in a foster home, or committed to a county ranch or school. The 601 ward could not be committed to the California Youth Authority (CYA), the youth version of the state prison system at the time. However, if a 601 ward violated the conditions of probation, the case could be referred back to court. This time the petition would be filed under Section 602, the delinquent category, alleging that the minor had violated a court order. The offense category, or legal status of the minor, would be **escalated** from status offender to law violator, and now the minor could be committed to CYA.

Usually, a 601 ward would be given several chances to "straighten out" before being committed to CYA. However, hundreds of juveniles were committed there over the years for conduct that never exceeded being incorrigible, runaway, or "...*being in danger of leading an idle, dissolute, lewd, or immoral life*." So many, in fact, that the California Youth Authority had a large network of institutions to provide for their *proper* training and treatment.

For example, Fricot School in the Sierras, housed the very young boys between ages 8 to 12. The girls' institutions, Los Guilicos and Ventura, held a number of escalated 601 wards, many
of whom had been charged with "...being in danger of leading an idle, dissolute, lewd, or immoral life." Los Guilicos, near Santa Rosa, held the younger girls, while Ventura was considered the "finishing school" that turned out real delinquents.

A Legal Challenge to the System

The constitutionality of the §601 phrase "...in danger of leading an idle, dissolute, lewd, or immoral life" was finally challenged in the case ***Gonzales v. Mailliard*, 1971**.

The circumstances of the case were derived from an incident that occurred on October 9, 1968, when two San Francisco police officers were assigned to investigate a report of an assault against a girl. The victim told the officers that she had been assaulted by about fifteen boys who were members of a local gang known as the *24th Street Gang*. She could only identify three of the boys by name.

The officers went to the area of 24th and Folsom Streets, where the gang hung out, and saw eight members there. Two of the boys identified by the victim also arrived at the scene. The officers arrested all ten boys, charging them with "...being in danger of leading an idle, dissolute, lewd, or immoral life" and on suspicion of robbery. However, all charges were soon dropped. Apparently, this was not the first time that police had used the §601 WIC statute to arrest members of this gang.

The plaintiffs (the boys) filed suit, and their argument by in support of their suit was the vagueness of the words "...*in danger of leading an idle, dissolute, lewd, or immoral life.*" They also claimed that the statute was used by police in a manner which denied them the First Amendment freedom of assembly. The court agreed and, in their review of the case, the three-judge panel noted their concern with "...the seriousness of the deprivation of freedom possible under Section 601...," and that a juvenile could end up in a camp or CYA as a result. The court also compared the language of Section 601 with the vague wording in adult vagrancy statutes which had been held unconstitutional. In addition, the court was concerned that the standard of proof necessary in criminal offenses, beyond a reasonable doubt, could be circumvented by police and other officials by using Section 601, which required less proof.

In the end, the court referred to the ***void-for-vagueness* doctrine** of the Supreme Court, and noted that the language in the law was so vague that it would be impossible to know what conduct to avoid or to prepare a defense against the offense described in such general abstract language.

The Court declared that portion of §601 in question unconstitutional and permanently enjoined the enforcement of it. That decision was appealed to the U.S.

Supreme Court by the defendants, where it was vacated and remanded back to the District Court for reconsideration of its decision (***Mailliard v. Gonzales, 1974***). However, by that time the California Legislature had removed the phrase "…in danger of..." from §601, effective in 1975, removing the entire issue from further consideration.

This decision marked an end of an era. Young boys and girls whose conduct was considered wayward or sinful, if you will, could no longer be locked up to be rehabilitated; to be saved from themselves, even if it meant turning them into sophisticated delinquents in the process. And, police or probation could no longer use the offense "…in danger of leading…" as a catch-all to control juvenile conduct that could not otherwise be stopped. The new procedure also had to be **retroactively applied**. That is, all 601 wards of the court, including those in institutions, had to be released and wardship terminated. It was not long before the CYA population decreased so much that several boys' camps and the Los Guilicos School for Girls were closed and sold.

The Traditional Approach Continued

It was business as usual in handling the other categories of status offenders. The processing of runaways, incorrigibles, and truants continued to be frequent and formal. They were considered "pre-delinquent "or displaying" pre-delinquent tendencies." Intervention was designed to save them and to change these dangerous tendencies before they developed into real delinquent acts.

The years between 1961 and 1976 are what this writer calls the *colonial period* in juvenile probation. Most every juvenile referred by police, parents, or schools was welcomed with opened arms and placed on some form of probation. As the caseloads increased, so did the need for probation officers. Jobs were plentiful and were filled by juvenile hall staff who were working to put themselves through college and saw the job of probation officer as a promotion. Some individuals took the job as a probation officer merely because they could not make the team in professional sports or because they could not decide what other career to follow.

Individual caseloads were a mixture of status offenders and delinquents. And, with the practice of escalating the 601s to 602s upon a violation of probation, the increasing intake of status offenders created a corresponding increase in 602s. Probation departments grew fat from an appetite that increased by what they fed on.

The Seeds of Revolution

In 1968, Congress passed the Juvenile Delinquency Prevention and Control Act, in which it recommended that minors charged with non-criminal acts (status offenders) be handled in some manner outside of the formal court system; but it was only a recommendation to the states.

Up until the mid to late 1960s, the so-called **medical model** pervaded the juvenile system. This was the view that delinquents had emotional problems that required psychiatric treatment and that their acting out behavior was symptomatic of those problems. It had been popular for 50 years, but was losing favor. It had not proven useful in dealing with juveniles.

This dissatisfaction combined with an increasing acceptance of a new idea, the **Labeling Theory**, a belief that if a juvenile is labeled delinquent long enough by those who shape his or her self-image, he or she eventually will accept and internalize the negative view and become delinquent. Thus, those who worked in the system came to believe that the practices of labeling the 601s as *pre-delinquent*, of telling them that they needed treatment, and of keeping them in the formal system and mixing them with delinquents, actually had created delinquents.

The new ethos in viewing status offenders was that *the sooner they came into the formal system, the deeper in they went, and the longer they stayed, the worse they became.* Many departments created **Diversion Units**. The 601s referred to the Hall were immediately diverted out of the system and, along with their families, underwent an intensive involvement based on **Family Systems Theory** - a newly popularized view that acting out behavior was symptomatic, not of emotional problems, but of a dysfunctional family and of family pain.

The juvenile was no longer considered the subject for change. The focus shifted to changing the set of relationships in which the juvenile was involved, namely the family patterns of communication and behavior.

Although California was a leader in a nationwide movement to get status offenders out of the system, federal legislation was the prime mover for everyone. In 1974, Congress passed **The Juvenile Justice and Delinquency Prevention Act** that established four custody-related requirements with which states must comply to qualify for federal funds related to delinquency programs. The requirement that directly affected status offenders stated that:

> ➤ **...deinstitutionalization** of status offenders (601s) requires that juveniles not charged with acts which would be crimes if committed by adults shall **not be detained in a secure facility.**

This requirement and the offer of federal funding provided the motivation for legislation in most states to deinstitutionalize status offenders. In fact, legislation in California and many other states moved beyond that requirement to completely divest status offenders from the formal juvenile justice system. The three additional requirements of the 1974 Act will be cited in Chapter 4, in the discussion of detaining juveniles in a law enforcement facility.

Summary

Prior to 1976, many status offenders were punished and abused by the juvenile justice system designed to save them from themselves; designed to treat them for their *own good* and to make them obedient. Many, in fact, were made worse.

The scarce resources of many law enforcement and probation agencies were often consumed by efforts that progressive thinkers came to believe could be better spent on dealing with serious delinquent problems, while community resources could better deal with family problems. The stage was set by the efforts and progressive practices of a few leaders and programs and by the impetus given by the promise of federal funding. The seeds of revolution were planted. This revolution was given final form and direction by legislation known as the Dixon Bill, detailed in the chapter that follows.

References

Dixon, Julian, "Juvenile Justice in Transition," *Pepperdine Law Review*, Vol. 4, No. 3 (1977).

Riback, Linda, "Juvenile Delinquency Laws: Juvenile Women and the Double Standard of Morality," *UCLA Law Review*, Vol. 19 (1971-72) pp. 313-342.

Roybal, Edward R., "Void for Vagueness: State Statutes Proscribing Conduct Only For a Juvenile," Pepperdine *Law Review*, Vol. 1, No. 1 (1973).

Saleebey, *George, Hidden Closets: A Study of Detention Practices in California*. Sacramento: California Youth Authority, 1975.

West, Mary Beth, "Juvenile Court Jurisdiction over Immoral Youth In California," *Pepperdine Law Review*, Vol. 1., No. 1(1973).

Internet references

http://www.cjcj.org/jjic/intro.php

Case Decisions

Gonzales v. Mailliard (1971) No. 50424, N.D. CA. The entire decision is reprinted in Appendix A of Pepperdine *Law Review*, Vol. 1, No.1 (1973).

Mailliard v. Gonzales (1974) 416 U. S. 918 (40 LEd.) 2d 276, 94 S.C.

Chapter 3: Current Status Offender Procedures

Key Terms and Concepts

AB 3121- the Dixon Bill	Missing persons procedures
At risk youth	Non-secure facility
Beyond control	Status offender
Curfew ordinance	Truancy procedures
Loitering ordinance	601 WIC

Introduction

This chapter examines the current procedures for responding to 601 behaviors, including **beyond control**, **runaway**, **truancy**, and **curfew**. It begins with an overview of legislation that revolutionized 601 procedures and, in the process, created an array of problems with which the justice community is still trying to cope and resolve. Police procedures with beyond control and runaway juveniles are reviewed, followed by a discussion of truancy and curfew procedures.

The Revolution of 1976

Assembly Bill (AB) 3121, known as the **Dixon Bill**, took effect in January 1976 as a response to reform efforts and to the 1974 federal legislation that provided funding for its compliance. It revolutionized juvenile procedures in four ways. Three of these will be discussed in the subsequent chapter on 602 delinquent procedures. The fourth way had a dramatic impact on how 601s could be handled, and is the focus of this chapter.

According to Dixon, the purpose of the bill was to **deinstitutionalize** the status offender. In fact, the bill amended §601 taking status offenders completely out of the formal system; and this was done almost overnight. Thus, the reason for using the term *revolution*.

The mandates of AB 3121:

> **prohibited the escalation of 601** petitions to 602 delinquent petitions based solely on a 601s failure to obey a court order. Consequently, no juvenile could be committed to a state institution without actually violating a Penal Code section
> removed curfew violations from §602 and inserted it under §601, thereby **decriminalizing curfew**
> **prohibited the detention of 601s** in secure facilities and the **mixing of 601s** with 602s in any context

Passage of the Dixon Bill meant that **status offenders could not be detained in a locked setting** such as a juvenile hall, camp, school, or ranch. In fact, a 601 could not be detained in any manner against his or her will. Those currently in detention in local or state facilities had to be released and returned home.

Instead of detention, 601s were to be housed temporarily in so-called crisis resolution homes or shelter care facilities on a voluntary basis. Of course, the state did not provide sufficient funding to establish such facilities. Some counties did and some did not, which is the situation today.

This means that the resources available to help in status offender situations depend on the county in which the parents happen to live. In effect, by enacting AB 3121, the Legislature threw the baby out with the bath water, and abandoned both juveniles and their parents to seek help in resolving family problems and teen problems from whatever private resources might be available.

The Current Section 601

The 1976, and current version of **Section 601 WIC** applied to any person under the age of 18 years who:

> persistently or habitually refuses to obey the reasonable and proper orders or directions of his parents, guardian, or custodian

> is **beyond the control, a runaway, or incorrigible**

> is under the age of 18 years when he or she violated any ordinance of any city or county of this state establishing a **curfew** based solely on age

> is an habitual **truant**

This definition was amended by SB 439 as of August 30 2018, to state any minor between the ages of 12 and 17 years, inclusive.

One might conclude from knowing the current §601 that it is still an offense for a minor to be **incorrigible**, to **run away**, or to **truant**. It is. A petition can be filed alleging that a juvenile is beyond the control of his or her parents or school, and the case can be processed through the court and the court may declare the minor a 601 ward, and place the minor on probation under orders not to commit any status offender behavior again. Initially, if the juvenile violates the court order, there was no sanction that can follow. The court was nearly impotent to enforce its orders because the status offender could not be detained against his or her will. Consequently, very few juveniles were referred to court as a 601.

Since the juvenile may not be detained in a secure facility, he or she may only be placed in an unlocked setting on a voluntary basis. Initially, most probation departments opened non-secure 601 housing units outside the fenced confines of their juvenile halls. California was one of the first states to decriminalize status offenses. Soon the word spread among the juveniles throughout the state, and even the nation, that runaway juveniles could not be detained in California. In no time at all, California became the runaway haven for juveniles; they came from all corners of the nation to enjoy the new-found freedom our law created.

The non-secure facilities became like free youth hostels. Juveniles could roam up and down the state, depending where the action was, and check into one of the 601 facilities when they were tired or hungry, re-fuel, plan activities with other runaways, and leave when they chose to. It was great for them, but it was a real financial drain on an already overloaded system. As a result, many probation departments quit the 601 business. They just hung out *No Vacancy* signs and refused to accept status offender.

The Impact of the Dixon Bill

It was stated earlier in Chapter 2 that before 1976, police involvement with status offenders was frequent and formal. Today, in many communities it is almost nonexistent, except to comply with the laws regarding missing persons, as discussed in a section below. The same can be said for the court and probation agencies.

One result is that there are thousands of juveniles roaming city streets today without any real place to live. They are the runaways and throwaways, and those who slip through the cracks because no one cares about them. It does not take much imagination to know what a 13, 14, 15, or 16-year-old boy or girl must resort to in order to survive: theft, drug sales, and prostitution. Drug abuse is prevalent, and AIDS is an increasing problem to which we are not prepared to respond. By 1998, 55 of 57 eligible states and territories had complied with the federal (1974) legislation and were participating in federal grant programs (Snyder and Sickmund, 1999, p. 88) that removed status offenders from the system. Today, thousands of *at-risk youths* roam the streets, highways, and byways of our nation.

Community Resources for 601s

Limited state and federal funds are available for the creation of community resources to assist status offenders and their families. It should be noted at this point that the phrase **at risk youth** is more appropriate than the phrase status offender. That takes the onus off the juvenile for any misconduct. Some state funds have been made available, but many local county commissions established to allocate the funds funneled off most of the money to county-run programs, which in turn minimized the help for many *at risk* juveniles.

In many counties today, funded non-profit organizations offer counseling services and/or temporary shelters for runaways. Often there is a fee for services but it is charged on a sliding scale according to one's ability to pay.

Law enforcement officers may pick up a runaway or incorrigible minor anywhere in the county and deliver him or her to a community program, if one is available. Of course, the minor is free to leave at any time, and any participation in counseling by the minor and/or the family is voluntary.

Recent Modifications in 601 Procedures

The intended consequences of removing status offenders from the formal justice system were accomplished quite easily in 1976 by the Dixon Bill. However, the unintended consequences of having juveniles wandering freely about the state at will, and leaving police and probation unable to help, created new problems equally as serious as the ones that were corrected.

In response to this, §207 WIC was amended in 1986, allowing probation authorities to detain a 601 in a juvenile facility (Hall) for:

- up to 12 hours to check on wants or warrants, if there is reason to believe that they might exist

- up to 24 hours to return the minor to his or her parents, if the parents reside within the state, and if they want the minor home, and if the minor wants to return home

- up to 72 hours to reunite a minor with out-of-state parents, if they and the minor want to reunite

This offers relief in some situations. However, if the parents or minor do not want to reunite, the minor is free to leave. Also, if the minor is temporarily detained by any probation agency, he or she may not have any contact with 602 delinquent minors. And, a 601 may not be detained in a law enforcement facility for any reason. Very few counties are prepared to comply with such requirements. Consequently, runaway or beyond control minors are rarely detained.

Missing Persons Procedures

Police procedures for responding to 601 behaviors have been complicated in recent years with the passage of missing persons legislation.

Section 14213 PC includes in the definition of a missing person:

...any child (minor under 18 years) who is missing voluntarily or involuntarily, or under circumstances not conforming to his or her ordinary habits or behavior and who may be in need of assistance.

It also includes any minor who may be *at risk*, which includes one who:
...may be the victim of a crime or foul play; is mentally retarded; may be the victim of parental abduction; or runs away, but has no pattern of running away or disappearing.

Section 14205 PC details the procedural requirements law enforcement agencies must follow in complying with the law:

> *§14205. Missing person reports*
> (a) All local police and sheriffs' departments shall accept any report, including any telephone report, of a missing person, including runaways, without delay and shall give priority to the handling of these reports over the handling of reports relating to crimes involving property.... In cases of reports involving missing persons,
>
> (b) including, but not limited to, runaways, the local police or sheriff's department shall immediately take the report and make an assessment of reasonable steps to be taken to locate the person. If the missing person is under 12 years of age, or if there is evidence that the person is *at risk*, the department shall broadcast a "Be On the Look-Out" bulletin, without delay, within its jurisdiction.
>
> (c) If the person reported missing is under 12 years of age, or if there is evidence that the person is *at risk*, the local police, sheriff's department, or the California Highway Patrol shall submit the report to the Attorney General's office within four hours after accepting the report...through the use of the California Telecommunications System.

Section 14206 PC elaborates on these procedures stating that the form used by law enforcement to take the missing persons report shall include a statement authorizing the release of the dental and/or skeletal x-rays of the missing person, and authorizing the release of a recent photograph of the person if under 18 years of age.

Instructions on the form state that if the person is still missing after 30 days, a family member or police officer shall take the release form to the respective dentist, doctor, or medical facility and obtain the x-rays. If no family member or next of kin exists or can be found, a law enforcement officer may complete a written declaration stating that said x-rays are necessary in conducting an active investigation into the location of a missing person. This is sufficient authority for the medical person to release the x-rays.

If the missing person is under age 18, and the law enforcement agency determines that the person is *at risk*, or if the person is under age 12 and has been missing at least 14 days, the completed release form or declaration shall be taken immediately to the appropriate medical persons.

Once x-rays have been obtained in each situation described above, the law enforcement agency shall confer with the county coroner or medical examiner, and shall submit its missing persons report and x-rays to the Attorney General's office. That information is then coded and entered into the computer of the state's Violent Crime Information Center and the National Crime Information Center (NCIC).

When a person is located, the locating agency shall immediately notify the Attorney General's office. When a missing child under age 12 or who is *at risk* is found, the report shall be made within 24 hours. The Attorney General's office shall then notify NCIC.

These procedures are designed to provide a coordinated state-wide capacity to identify and locate missing persons, especially children, as soon as possible after they are missed. The efforts during the first few days are critical in finding an *at-risk* youth who might be the victim of abduction or foul play.

601 Truancy Procedures

Section 601 was modified again effective January 2, 2000 to add a number of subsections in an effort to curb truancy and the types of delinquency that result, such as daytime burglaries. This is not just a statewide concern. Many communities across the nation are enacting ordinances to curb truancy. Similar efforts are underway nationwide to curb delinquency by enacting curfew and loitering ordinances similar to those discussed below.

In addition to the description of truancy stated in §601 cited in the beginning of this chapter, §601(b) also was modified to read as follows:

> ➤ If a minor has been declared an habitual truant by a school attendance review board or truancy mediation program (a process beyond the scope of this work), and has been referred to the Probation Officer, a 601 petition may be filed, and, upon a finding of truancy, the court may declare the minor a ward. The minor may then be removed from the custody of his or her parents during school hours and detained in a secure school setting.

Generally speaking, this is another empty code section because few, if any, counties will spend resources on implementing any of these alternatives allowed by the law. Consequently, truancy usually results in the minor's referral to some sort of continuation school or expulsion from school. The parents, of course, can be prosecuted criminally for violating Education Code Section 48293 for allowing their child to truant. However, in most cases, the child is beyond the control of the parents at this point, and prosecution of them will have little effect.

Sections 601.1 to 601.5 detail an elaborate process in which counties may create **At-Risk Youth Early Intervention Programs** which shall establish **Youth Referral Centers** to interface with truant and troubled youths, their families, the court, and probation. These centers are to provide family assessments and counseling, and a lack of cooperation by a juvenile referred could lead to a 601 petition being filed on behalf of the minor. A 601-truancy petition can be filed and sustained, and the court may declare the juvenile a ward and order him or her to attend school as a condition of probation.

If the juvenile violates that condition, the court may find the juvenile in contempt of court and order him or her detained in a secure facility to insure school attendance (***In re Michael G., 1988***). The juvenile would have to be housed separately from any 602s.

This would be a costly process. Consequently, few county governments will spend the money. Some do, however. The reader might check with his or her local agencies to ascertain their procedures of handling truants.

There is **one police procedure** for dealing with the casual truant that can be effective. Sections 48200-48232 of the California Education Code require children between the ages of 6 to 18 years to be in school during school hours. Section 48264 states that:

> … a peace officer may arrest or assume temporary custody, during school hours, of any minor subject to compulsory full-time education…found away from his or her home and who is absent from school without a valid excuse….

In the case *In re* **James Edward D., 1987** the Supreme Court upheld this authority of police to stop any person who looks to be of school age in order to determine if that person belongs in school. The Court held that the social benefits of such a procedure outweigh any restraint of individual freedom that might be involved in such a stop.

Municipal ordinances have been passed in many cities to include truancy in a broad curfew law. Truants, in addition to being returned to school, are being cited to (Probation) traffic court, where they can be fined, and the fine can affect their eligibility to obtain a driver license.

Police Searches of Truants

The issue of police searches during truancy stops was clarified by the Second DCA on April 24, 2000, in the case of *In re* **Humberto**. Three Los Angeles police officers were on juvenile patrol in Hollywood and observed Humberto walking down the street at about 9:15 a.m. on a weekday, several miles from Hollywood High School. They stopped and detained him because of the time of day, his youthful appearance, a backpack he carried, and the proximity to school.

Officers verified that he was a truant and told him that they would cite him for truancy and return him to school. Before cuffing the minor and placing him in the car, officers pat searched him and searched his backpack, where they found a dagger.

Officers then changed his custody status from truancy to a violation of §12020 PC, felony possession of a dirk or dagger.

A petition was filed in juvenile court alleging this offense and the minor's attorney immediately moved to suppress the knife as the fruit of an unlawful search. The juvenile court agreed with the motion and dismissed the petition. The People appealed to the Second DCA. The appellate court reversed the juvenile court's decision and held that:

> ➤ It is settled Fourth Amendment doctrine that a police officer may, incident to a lawful arrest, conduct a contemporaneous warrantless search of the arrestee's person and of the area into which the arrestee might reach to retrieve a weapon or destroy evidence.

The appellate court equated the minor's temporary §601 custody status as a truant with the arrest status of an adult, giving officers the authority to search, incident to temporary custody of a minor. (***People v. Ingham*, 1992**)

601 Curfew/Loitering Procedures

An increasing number of counties and cities are enacting curfew or curfew/loitering ordinances for juveniles in order to suppress gang activities and other juvenile offenses. The Bakersfield city ordinance serves as a good example. Its ordinance provided that:

> ➤ It is unlawful for any person under the age of eighteen years to loiter upon the streets of the city, in places of amusement or entertainment, or in other public places within the city, between the hours of ten p. m. and five a. m. of any day unless such person is accompanied by a parent, guardian or other adult person having control or charge of such person under the age of eighteen years: or unless such person under the age of eighteen years has gone to a place of entertainment or amusement other than one at which liquor is sold or served, prior to eight p. m., where a regular program of entertainment has commenced or been arranged for the occasion to commence prior to eight p. m., and had held over or been continued beyond ten p. m., and such person is thereafter returning

directly to his or her home or place of residence in a reasonable manner (Bakersfield Mun. Code, # 9.44.010: Ord. No. 3188, S.1.)

This ordinance is a useful example, not only for its description of prohibited behavior, but because it was appealed in California as unconstitutionally *void-for-vagueness* and unreasonably restrictive. Also, it is a good example of a situation in which a police officer, acting in good faith and under lawful authority in his belief that a city ordinance was legal, made a search incident to an arrest and found contraband. Consequently, the events and appellate decision are worth noting below.

The case of In re Daniel D., 1995

On April 2, 1994, Officer Martin Herdia observed five youths standing on a Bakersfield city sidewalk at about 10:55 p.m. He approached one of the youths, Daniel D., and asked him his age. When Daniel said that he was 15 years old, Officer Herdia took him into temporary custody (arrest) for violating the loitering ordinance. Herdia knew this area was a hangout and cruising spot for juveniles and knew there were no places of entertainment or bus stops in the area. It seemed obvious to Officer Herdia that Daniel was not coming or going anywhere and was not in the company of his parents. After the arrest Officer Herdia searched Daniel and found a loaded .38-caliber handgun in his right front pants pocket.

At his adjudication hearing (juvenile trial), Daniel's attorney moved to suppress the handgun and ammunition as fruits of an illegal search. The motion was denied because the court concluded that the officer could assume, based on his experience and the ***totality of the circumstances***, that Daniel was in violation of the city ordinance and, therefore, the search incident to arrest was legal. Daniel was adjudicated a delinquent for possession of a concealed weapon and possession of live ammunition (§12101 PC) without his parent's permission, as well as car theft an offense he had committed earlier.

Daniel appealed to the 5th District Court of Appeal (DCA), claiming that the loitering ordinance unreasonably interferes with the exercise of personal rights by being too broad and discriminatory; that it was *void-for-vagueness* because it provides no notice of the behavior prohibited; and that it provides no guidelines to govern its enforcement by police.

The DCA ruled against Daniel, explaining that the constitutional standard applicable to a juvenile curfew ordinance is one of *reasonableness*:

> ➢ When an ordinance is attacked as unduly restrictive of personal rights, the test is whether the ordinance is reasonable, in view of **the needs of the state,** with reasonableness being roughly measured by the gravity of the evil to be corrected and the importance of the right invaded.

In its opinion, the court cited other case decisions that have recognized the state's need to regulate juvenile behavior for the protection of both the juvenile and the community (see, ***In re* Nancy C., 1972** and ***People v. Walton*, 1945**).

The Fifth DCA's decision was appealed to the State Supreme Court, and in August 1995, the Court agreed to hear the case. However, on January 18, 1996, the Supreme Court reversed itself, said the hearing was granted in error, dismissed the appeal, and let stand the decision by the 5th DCA.

Ordinances in Reedly, Bellflower, Long Beach, and the County of Santa Clara are other examples of **curfew/loitering laws** designed to suppress delinquency. Enforcement varies between jurisdictions. Police in Bakersfield, for example, take the minor to the police station and have him or her wait in the lobby for his or her parents.

Summary

Limited resources exist today to help juveniles or parents get through those critical teen years.

The few resources available would include the At-Risk Early Intervention Programs and Youth Referral Centers established by the modification of Sections 601.1 to 601.5 WIC to deal with truancy and family problems. Nevertheless, today an increasing number of juveniles are running away, and the age of the runaways seems to be getting younger every day.

Legislation and procedures for missing persons and truancy were detailed, as was the use of curfew/loitering ordinances, all designed to resolve the problems created by removing the formal and legal controls that had been the traditional way of responding to status offender behavior since we devised a juvenile justice system.

It was noted that truancy and anti-loitering ordinances are being used with increasing frequency as the primary intervention device for police seeking to prevent and control gang violence and other juvenile offenses. We also noted that when a court decision supported these efforts, it gave strong support to the state's need to regulate juvenile behavior for the protection of both the juvenile and the community. In judging of the restrictions on personal liberty of juveniles imposed by loitering ordinances, the U.S. Supreme Court balanced the "…gravity of the evil to be corrected… (with)…the importance of the right invaded…" and the needs of the state (*parens patriae*) to correct the evil, prevailed.

One would not want to return to the severity of the pre-1976 procedures, but surely more changes are needed to help the *at-risk* youths, provide resources for their parents, and to protect the community.

References

Dixon, Julian, "Juvenile Justice in Transition," *Pepperdine Law Review*, Vol. 4, No. 3 (1977).

Lemert, Edwin M. *Social Action and Legal Change: Revolution with the Juvenile Court*. Chicago: Aldine, 1970.

Roybal, Edward R., "Void for Vagueness: State Statutes Proscribing Conduct Only For a Juvenile," Pepperdine *Law Review*, Vol. 1, No. 1 (1973).

Snyder, Howard N., and Melissa Sickmund. *Juvenile Offenders and Victims: 1999 National Report*. Washington, D.C.: Office of Juvenile Justice and Delinquency Prevention.

Internet References

http://www.thelegaldictionary.com/legal-term-details/Status-Offenders

http://www.ncjrs.gov/html/ojjdp/publist2000/status.html

http://www.ojjdp.ncjrs.org/pubs/gender/

http://www.buildingblocksforyouth.org/issues/jjdpa/factsheet.html

Case Decisions

In re Daniel D. (1995) 24 Cal. App 4th 1823

In re Humberto (2000) 2nd DCA (4/25/2000, B128478)

In re James D. (1987) 43 Cal. 3d 903; 239 Cal. Rptr, 663.

In re Michael G. (1988) 44 Cal. 283 Cal. Rptr. 224.

In re Nancy C. (1972) 28 Cal. App 3d 747, 75

People v. Ingham (1992) 5 Cal. App. 4th 326

People v. Walton (1945) 70 Cal. App 2d Supp. 862-8

Chapter 4: Police Procedures with Law Violators

Key Terms and Concepts

Arrest	Functional specialization
Consensual encounter	In-field show-up
Consent search	Non-secure custody
Delinquency	Patsearch
Delinquent	Probable (reasonable) cause
Detention	Reasonable suspicion
Detention petition	Secure custody (detention)
Discretion	Taken into temporary custody
Discretionary factors	Ward of the court
	Youth Service Bureau

Introduction

This chapter deals with the procedures that law enforcement officers must and/or may follow when handling juvenile law violators. We move from the point of first contact on the street by a law enforcement officer, either by consensual encounter, lawful detention, or arrest, through the law enforcement custody phases to the moment when police terminate their involvement, either by dismissal or by referral to another agency.

To reiterate, this chapter deals only with the law and procedures concerning the suspected delinquent, the **law violator**.

Functional Specialization

Police work is often organized around the concept known as **functional specialization**. That is, the total of all the work to be performed by the agency is divided into specialized functional categories. The larger the organization, the more specialized the work assignments become and the more an officer performs only one small function. Consequently, some organizations have work divisions or units that handle specialized matters relating to juveniles, such a Youth Services Division, a Gang Intelligence Unit, a Runaway Unit, Youth Outreach School Liaison Unit, a Child Abuse Investigation Unit, a Narcotics Unit, a Missing Persons Unit, and perhaps a Juvenile Diversion Unit.

Many of California's law enforcement agencies are small, and specialization is either not possible or desirable. One officer might perform patrol work and traffic enforcement, while at the same time serve on the SWAT team, and work both street narcotics and vice. These officers are generalists and deal with both adults and juveniles in a whole array of offense situations.

There is no longer a clear distinction between adult gangs and juvenile gangs. Frequently, there are just gangs with members of different ages. Consequently, there is a move away from having special juvenile gang officers in certain situations. These have been replaced by the use of gang task forces composed of officers from various agencies, such as city police, county sheriff, and county probation, who work together to suppress gang activities.

Delinquency: A Legal Definition

Section 602 of the Welfare and Institutions Code describes the juvenile law violator as amended by SB 439 on August 30, 2018:

> ➢ Any person who is between 12 and 17 years, inclusive, when he violates any law of this state or of the United States or any ordinance of any city or county of this state defining crime other than an ordinance establishing a curfew based solely on age, is within the jurisdiction of the juvenile court, which may adjudge such person to be a ward of the court. (The bill provides **an exception** for minors ages 12 and under who commit murder and four other specified violent sex crimes.)

A delinquent then, is **a minor between 12 and 17 who commits an act that would be a crime if committed by an adult**. The words here are carefully chosen. Juveniles do not commit crimes, they commit delinquent acts. They can enter and exit the system as a juvenile offender and never receive a criminal conviction in the process.

The wording of the laws and procedures that follow are unique to the juvenile justice system and still reflect the **protective philosophy** that has always been the hallmark of juvenile procedures. It is important that one learn the vocabulary to understand how the law and procedures operate.

Any reader planning to seek employment within the juvenile justice system or law enforcement would do well to know and understand Sections 601 to 608 and 625 to 641 of the Welfare and Institutions code (WIC). They detail the procedural requirements necessary in dealing with minors.

Police - Juvenile Transactions

In his written opinion in the case *Florida v. Royer, 1983*, U. S. Supreme Court Justice Byron White observed that police contact with juveniles occurs at three different levels of legal authority, just as they do with adults, ranging from the least to the most intrusive. We shall examine below the elements of each level.

Consensual Encounter

The first level is what Justice White termed a **consensual encounter** which is defined as a *transaction between a peace officer and a minor that are by the consent of both parties*. Their exchanges may continue until one or both decide to end them. The officer might have a gut feeling that the minor is up to some sort of illegal activity, but the officer does not have the reasonable suspicion based on facts, observations, and experience that allows him or her to detain the minor.

The officer may ask questions, or ask permission to examine something, such as the trunk of a car, but the minor is free to leave, free not to answer, and free to decline permission for a search. However, the juvenile is not usually aware of his or her position and submits to any search. Knowing this, police often use the **consent search** as a method of gaining access to search areas that they otherwise have no legal basis to enter.

The Detention

The second level of interaction between a law enforcement officer and a juvenile is what Justice White described as a legal **detention**. The minor is not in custody, but is not free to leave.

The officer's authority is based on a **reasonable suspicion** that:

➢ some delinquent activity has taken place, or is occurring, or is about to occur

➢ the minor either was involved, is involved, or is preparing to become involved in a delinquent offense

The officer's temporary seizure of the juvenile, however, is limited in scope, duration, and purpose. The officer's *reasonable suspicion* must be based on facts, observations, and experience that would cause any reasonable police officer in a like position to arrive at the same suspicion (***In re* Tony C., 1978**).

The concept of reasonableness is not an absolute, it is relative to the situation at hand. For example, if a patrol officer is advised by dispatch that an offense just occurred and a description of the suspect is given, and the officer observes a minor, who matches that description, running down the street near the scene, the officer's suspicion would be reasonable and a detention would be legal. The officer would have the legal authority to detain the minor until his or her suspicions are settled one way or the other.

If at some point during the detention process the officer has reasonable suspicion that the minor might be armed, the officer may conduct a **patsearch** of the minor, merely to look for weapons to insure the safety of the officer. Hunches and hearsay do not count in forming a reasonable basis for suspicion

If the officer pats an object in the minor's pocket, he can retrieve the object only if it reasonably resembles the size, shape, or feel of a weapon (***Terry v. Ohio, 1968***). This so-called ***Terry doctrine*** was made applicable to juvenile procedures in 1970 (***In re* Glenn R.**).

The standard for determining a law enforcement detention was stated by Justice Stewart in a second opinion included in a U. S. Supreme Court case (***U. S. v. Mendenhall*, 1980**) as follows:

➢ A person has been "seized" within the meaning of the Fourth Amendment only if, in view of all the circumstances surrounding the incident, a reasonable person would have believed that he was not free to leave.

If an officer finds evidence of an offense during an illegal detention, or patdown search, it falls under a legal doctrine called the exclusionary rule and is inadmissible in court.

A victim identification procedure known as the **in-field show-up** often comes into play at this point. This is used when police have reasonable suspicion to detain a minor shortly after an offense has occurred, and often in the general location of the offense. The minor will be detained in public view by one officer and another officer will drive by with the victim or witness to observe the minor. Usually, this will clear up the officer's suspicion one way or the other, and the minor will either be released or taken into custody. It is important that the officers do not suggest in any way to the victim or witness that an actual suspect is in custody or is detained.

The third level of a police - juvenile transaction is an arrest.

Police Authority to Arrest

The term arrest is used here initially only because most readers will have a common knowledge of what it means. However, an *arrest* refers to a procedure police use with adults. With juveniles, the term arrest sounds too harsh. For years, the preferred phrase has been ***take into temporary custody***. Like many phrases in juvenile procedures, this one sounds softer and more protective, whereas arrest sounds not only harsh, but punitive as well. In recent years, however, law enforcement, politicians, and the media have moved away from using the softer terms as a reflection of a *get-tough* attitude toward juveniles.

Police derive their authority from three subsections of §625 WIC:

A peace officer may, without a warrant, take into temporary custody a minor:
- a) who is under the age of 18 years when such officer has **reasonable cause (probable cause)** for believing that such minor is a person described in Sections 601 or 602
- b) who is a ward of the juvenile court or concerning whom an order has been made under Sections 636 or 702, when such officer has **reasonable cause** for believing that person has violated an order of the juvenile court or has escaped from any commitment ordered by the juvenile court

c) who is under the age of 18 years and who is found in any street or public place **suffering** from any sickness or injury which requires care, medical treatment, hospitalization, or other remedial care

The code does not distinguish here between felony and misdemeanor when referring to the officer's authority because any law violation is a delinquent act. Consequently, a misdemeanor does not have to be committed in the officer's presence as it does for adults. For example, when a police officer responds to a store where a minor is being detained by store security for shoplifting, the officer takes the minor into temporary custody based on the reasonable cause provided by the report of security personnel. Then the officer has full legal control over the case and has discretion on how to proceed with the juvenile. The same authority applies whenever a police officer takes custody of a minor from another party, such as a school administrator or a private person.

Under §625(b) WIC, the phrase *ward of the court* refers to a minor currently on county probation or state parole. Law enforcement officers on patrol routinely encounter court wards during traffic stops or other detention situations. If the officer radios for a record check on the minor and the report comes back showing wardship as the status, the record will usually show the probation or parole conditions. If the officer has reasonable cause to believe that the minor is in violation of any probation condition, the officer may take the minor into temporary custody.

Once a minor has been taken into temporary custody other code sections detailed below dictate what procedures the officer may or shall follow. With one exception an officer has complete discretion as to which disposition to make.

Police Options after Taking Custody of a Minor

After a police officer has taken a minor into temporary custody by the authority given in §625 WIC, the officer must advise the minor of his or her right to remain silent and to have an attorney present during any questioning. This is required **for both 601s and 602s taken into custody**. The details of this legal requirement are presented in Chapter 5. Assume at this point that the minor in custody has been advised of his or her rights, as required under California law.

Next, the officer must choose from one of four actions (dispositions) prescribed in §626 WIC:
- ➤ release the minor
- ➤ divert the minor to a program
- ➤ cite and release the minor
- ➤ deliver the minor to the local juvenile hall

Release the Minor

A peace officer may release the minor whenever and wherever he or she deems it appropriate. The officer may take the minor home and discuss the situation with the parents, release him or her at the station, or release him or her at the scene.

No further action will be taken by the officer, although a record of the field contact will be made.

Divert the Minor

An officer may refer or personally deliver a minor to an agency with which the city or county has an agreement or plan to provide shelter care, counseling, or diversion services to minors. Referral agencies have been established in many cities and counties to provide such services.

Some police agencies actually refer juveniles to their own in-house diversion program or Youth Service Bureau (YSB). The juvenile appears at the police or sheriff's station with his or her parents and meets with staff to discuss a disposition. The operation of these YSBs is not standardized throughout the state. In some instances, police officers meet with the family. In other agencies professional counseling staff meet and handle the matter. The juvenile is given the choice of admitting the offense and participating in the program or having the officer follow a more formal option. The disposition often includes some period of so-called police probation, restitution to the victim, an apology to the victim, community service work, and counseling. These in-house YSBs, however, are expensive and are falling out of favor with many law enforcement agencies.

Cite and Release

Under this option, an officer will prepare a written notice (citation) to appear before the county probation officer at a time and place identified on the notice. It shall also include a statement about why the minor was taken into temporary custody; a summary of the offense. The officer shall give one copy of the citation to the minor or a parent, guardian, or responsible adult, and the officer may require both the minor and/or a parent to sign the citation as a *promise to appear* as directed.

Deliver to a Juvenile Hall

The wording of the code is "Take the minor without unnecessary delay before the probation officer of the county...." This actually means to take the minor to the local juvenile hall. This can be the Hall in either the county in which the minor was taken into temporary custody, where the offense occurred, or where the minor lives.

The court in any of these counties can have jurisdiction, which is different from adult procedures in which the offender is booked in jail in the county where the crime occurred. Usually, the minor is taken to the Hall in the county in which he or she is apprehended, proceedings are initiated, and then the minor's case is transferred to the county of residence.

In deciding which of these four alternatives to choose, the W & I Code states again that the officer "...**shall prefer the alternative which least restricts the minor's freedom of movement**, provided that alternative is compatible with the best interests of the minor and the community." This gives the officer wide discretion to choose which option is best suited to the minor's individual situation, regardless of the offense, with **one exception**, as described below.

This exception is detailed in the new **Gang Violence and Juvenile Crime Prevention Act**, as introduced in Chapter 1. Section 625.3 WIC was amended to read:

> ➤ Notwithstanding Section 625, a minor who is 14 years of age or older and who is taken into custody by a peace officer for the **personal use of a firearm** in the commission or attempted commission of a felony or any offense listed in subdivision (b) of Section 707 **shall not** be released until that minor is brought before a judicial officer.

This new subsection was effective March 8, 2000, and takes all discretion away from a peace officer who takes a minor into custody in any situation described by §625.3. These are the serious and violent offenses listed in §707(b) WIC, in which a minor personally uses a firearm in the commission or attempted commission of the offense.

In these cases, **the officer shall take the minor to the juvenile hall**, where a probation officer or the court can decide to release or detain the minor for further proceedings.

Police Interrogation of Minors

Once a minor age 15-years or under is taken into temporary custody, he or she may not be questioned about an offense without the minor first consulting with an attorney, and that consultation may be either in person, by phone, or via teleconference. A minor cannot waive that requirement. A minor age 14 or under may not be questioned unless it can be shown that he or she understands right from wrong and knows that the offense was wrong.

Law enforcement may question a child age 15 or younger *before* the child has consulted with a lawyer if:

1. The officer reasonably believes the information is necessary to protect life or property from an imminent threat, **AND**

2. The officer's questions are limited to those that are reasonably necessary to obtain that information.

By way of information at this point, it is noted that as of January 2019, minors ages 15 and under cannot be referred to criminal court for prosecution as adults. They will remain under the jurisdiction of the juvenile court regardless of the offense.

Factors Influencing Discretion

A number of factors will be considered by an officer in choosing which disposition to make. The cost of each option is a serious consideration. It is far cheaper to cite a minor than to deliver him or her to the hall, especially when the results might be the same. If a minor is taken to the juvenile hall, a probation officer will review the minor's case and the need to keep the minor detained. That officer must consider certain specific factors in reaching a decision, and if those factors are not present, he or she must release the minor.

Consequently, it is suggested herein that the police officer consider those same factors, which are:

- Is the minor's home fit?
- Is there a parent or responsible adult available to provide supervision?
- Is the minor likely to flee the jurisdiction?
- Is the minor a danger to self or others?
- Is the minor currently on probation or parole?
- Was a firearm used in the alleged offense?

If the answers to these are *no*, it might be a waste of time and money to take the minor to the Hall because he or she probably will be released soon by the probation officer, and this will be a source of frustration for the arresting officer.

Other factors will be considered by the police: seriousness of the offense, risk to the community, attitude of the minor toward the offense or victim, department policy, available community resources, and many more. The attitude of the minor toward the officer will undoubtedly be a factor considered by many officers, even though it is not a predictor of future conduct, and it allows the situation to become personal, rather than remaining professional.

Detained Minor's Right to Make Phone Calls

When a peace officer takes a minor into temporary custody under the authority of §625 WIC, and takes the minor to a place of confinement, the officer **shall immediately** advise the minor that he or she has the right to complete two phone calls. And, except where physically impossible, the minor shall be so advised within one hour of being taken into custody, and shall be allowed to complete the calls. One call may be to an attorney, and one to a parent, guardian, or responsible adult (§627 WIC). Any officer or public employee who willfully deprives a minor of this right is guilty of a misdemeanor. A place of confinement refers to either a police station where the minor is held or a juvenile hall.

Voluntary Chemical Testing of Minors

Any 602 minor taken into temporary custody under the authority of §625 WIC may be asked to submit to a chemical test for the purpose of determining the presence of alcohol or illegal drugs. The peace officer shall inform the minor that the test is voluntary and that the minor has the right to telephone his or her parent or guardian before deciding whether or not to take this test.

As in the case of any waiver situation, the minor must acknowledge that he or she understands those rights and must then either invoke the protection or knowingly and intelligently waive the rights and submit to testing. At this point the minor is already in custody for an offense. If the test comes back positive, the results cannot be used to add another offense, but only in the dispositional hearing (sentencing), or a violation of probation hearing, when the judge decides what type of treatment is best suited for the minor.

A police officer who stops a minor and finds a sufficient amount of blood-alcohol, may take the minor's driver license immediately and issue him a temporary one good for thirty days. A report of the offense is made by the police to DMV, who will review the facts and may suspend the minor's driver license for one year. Failure to submit to a blood-alcohol test by a minor results in an automatic suspension of the minor's driver license for one year.

Custody of Minors in Law Enforcement Facility

In 1986, the California Legislature passed SB 1637, effective January 1, 1988, modifying WIC Sections 207.1, 209, 210.2 and 1712, to create standards for the temporary detention of minors in law enforcement facilities. This would bring them into compliance with the federal Juvenile Justice and Delinquency Prevention Act of 1974, discussed in Chapter 2. The three requirements of that act responded to by this WIC legislation were:

> ➤ juveniles alleged to have committed any delinquent act (602s) **shall not be detained in any facility where they have sight or sound contact with any adult**

> **no juvenile shall be held in an adult jail or lockup** facility (except those pending adult prosecution per §777 and held in jail per a court finding and order). Also, 602 juveniles detained in a police facility **shall not be detained longer than six hours**

> **no disproportionate confinement** of minority youth in local facilities; and states shall examine their facilities to determine the existence and extent of the problem and demonstrate efforts to reduce it where it exists

Initially, the State Division of Juvenile Facilities (formerly known as the California Youth Authority) was given the responsibility of developing the standards and monitoring the law enforcement agencies to assure compliance. Currently, the State Board of Corrections provides these monitoring services. These standards were adopted effective March 25, 1988, and provide the legal guidance for law enforcement agencies and officers in detaining minors.

Before we examine those standards, it will be useful to define the relevant terms used in the law

> the term **law enforcement facility** refers to a police or sheriff's office or station, other than a county jail or detention facility that holds pretrial or sentenced adult prisoners

> **temporary custody** means that the minor is not free to leave the facility

> **non-secure custody** means that the minor is not locked in or physically secured, but that the minor's freedom of movement is controlled by staff and the minor is under constant personal visual observation and supervision by staff

> **secure custody** means that the minor is locked in a room enclosure and/or is physically secured to a cuffing rail or other stationary object

Current law states that any minor taken into temporary custody by a peace officer on the basis that he or she is a person described in §602 WIC and who, in the reasonable belief of the peace officer, presents a serious security risk of harm to self or others, may be held in either secure detention or non-secure detention within a law enforcement facility that contains a lockup for adults for **up to six hours**, provided that certain specific standards are met.

Secure Detention in a Locked Room

A minor held in **secure detention** shall be age 14 years or older and must present a security risk of harm to self or others. He or she shall be informed at the time of said detention why he or she is securely detained, the length of time detention is expected to last, and the maximum time that the detention may last. The maximum time for detention within the police facility is **six (6) hours**, regardless of the circumstances. A minor may be held in secure detention or otherwise reasonably restrained as necessary to prevent escape and protect the minor and others from harm.

The place where the minor is detained shall meet all the applicable health, safety, and fire requirements; shall have seats for the minor in the form of chairs or benches; and shall have adequate ventilation and lighting.

Minors placed in secure detention shall be provided the blankets and clothing necessary to assure the comfort of the minor. However, the minor shall be allowed to wear his or her personal clothing unless it is inadequate, presents a health problem, or is needed as evidence of an offense.

Minors detained in a locked room shall have adequate supervision, which includes constant auditory access to staff by the minor and unscheduled personal visual observation by staff at least every thirty minutes. Male and female juveniles shall not be locked in the same room or enclosure unless under constant visual observation by staff.

If a minor is securely detained outside of a locked room or enclosure by being handcuffed to a cuffing rail or other stationary object, the minor shall not be handcuffed for longer than 30 minutes, and while handcuffed, a staff person shall be present at all times to assure the minor's safety. That means thirty minutes total time, not thirty minutes at a time.

Non-secure Detention

Minors who do not meet the criteria for secure detention specified in Section 207.1 WIC (who are under age 14 years and/or who do not present a risk) must be held in **non-secure detention** within the facility. A minor so held shall receive constant personal visual observation and supervision by staff. **Remember**, no 601 may be detained in a law enforcement facility for any purpose. A 602 minor may be held in temporary custody **only** for:

> **the purposes of investigating the case**

> **facilitating release of the minor to a parent or guardian**

> **arranging transfer of the minor to an appropriate juvenile hall**

The time for any such **detention**, again, **cannot exceed six hours**.

The facility in which the minor is detained shall have approved written policies and procedures specifically concerning minors held in temporary custody that shall address discipline, suicide risk and prevention, uses of restraints, and medical assistance and services. Any minor held in temporary detention shall have the following made available:

> reasonable access to drinking water, toilets and washing facilities

> privacy during visitations with family, guardian, and/or attorney

> a snack if the minor has not eaten within the past four hours, or is otherwise in need of nourishment

This regulation requiring privacy during visitations does not mean that the minor has the reasonable expectation of absolute privacy within a law enforcement facility during conversations between a minor and his or her parents. If the conversation takes place in an interrogation room, not a visiting room, the expectation of privacy is not guaranteed. The only completely privileged conversations are between a minor and an attorney.

The final regulation states that during any period of detention, the peace officer shall exercise one of the dispositional options authorized under Sections 626 and 626.5 WIC without unnecessary delay. And, regardless of the circumstances, **a minor shall**

not be detained in the facility for longer than six (6) hours. The time begins when the minor enters the police facility and ends when he or she leaves the facility.

Summary

In this chapter, we began with a legal definition of §602 and the delinquent in California, we detailed the procedures that law enforcement officers must use when encountering juveniles in the various types of contact: consensual encounter, detention, and temporary custody (arrest).

We examined the authority of police, including their discretion, and the four dispositional options they have when dealing with minors suspected of offenses, and we detailed the legal requirements for handling the detention or temporary custody of minors in law enforcement facilities. In today's economy, the availability of assigning officers to special juvenile work units will depend on the priorities of the community and of law enforcement agencies.

References

Phelps, Thomas R. *Juvenile Delinquency: A Contemporary View.* Pacific
    Palisades: Goodyear, 1976.
Shepherd, Robert E. Jr., "Juvenile Identification Practices and Procedures,"
    American Bar Association Journal of Criminal Justice, Vol. 5, No. 4 (Winter
    1991), pp. 44-46.

Internet References

http://www.lapdonline.org/juvenile_division
www.ncgccd.org/PDFs/JuvJus/Chart.pdf

http://www.unicri.it/wwk/documentation/lmsdb.php?kw_=POLICE%20JUVENILE%20SERVICES

http://www.cpcachiefs.org/chiefs/research/juvenile.html

https://leginfo.legislature.ca.gov/faces/codes_displayexpandedbranch.xhtml?tocCode=WIC&division=2.&title=&part=&chapter=&article=

Case Decisions

Florida v. Royer (1983) 460 U. S. 491

In re Gladys R., 1 Cal.3d 855 (1970)

In re Glenn R. (1970) 7 CA 3d 558; 86 Cal. Rptr. 366

In re Tony C. (1978) 21 Cal. 3d 888

Terry v. Ohio (1968) 329 U. S. 1

U. S. v. Mendenhall (1980) 446 U. S. 544

Chapter 5: Special Law Enforcement Procedures

Key Terms and Concepts

Administrative search	Gang registration	Reasonable suspicion
Criminal street gang	Gang suppression	Scope of a search
Custodial-interrogation	Independent state grounds	Search clause
Enhancement time		Section 625 WIC
Exclusionary Rule	Interested adult laws	Section 627 WIC
Fifth Amendment	Jumping-in	Sixth Amendment
FourthAmendment	Miranda warning	Standing
Gang certification	Probation search	STEP Act
Gang checkpoint	Proposition 21	
Gang crimes	Parole search	

Introduction

This chapter examines three special procedural areas that law enforcement officers encounter on a daily basis:

- the Fifth and Sixth Amendment protections for juveniles
- the Fourth Amendment protection for juveniles
- the suppression of juvenile gang activities

Each procedural area will be considered independent of the other two, and will be examined in the order indicated above.

Fifth and Sixth Amendment Protections

For adults, the Fifth and Sixth Amendment protections refer to an individual's **right to remain silent** in the face of police custodial interrogation and the **right to have an attorney** present during questioning, and at all stages of a criminal proceeding. For juveniles, these rights take on another dimension in that the juvenile might need additional protection beyond what is necessary for an adult.

The Miranda Requirement

These Fifth and Sixth Amendment advisements are referred to by some as the *Miranda* warning. However, that is a misnomer. *Miranda* is a requirement under federal case law (***Miranda v. Arizona, 1966***), binding on the states, which applies during custodial interrogation. The requirement under
California law that police must follow when dealing with juveniles is found in **WIC §625(b).** This law requires law enforcement officers to **advise any minor taken into temporary custody** of his or her constitutional rights, regardless of what disposition the officer might subsequently make.

However, by complying with the requirements of California law, an officer will have met any requirements under *Miranda*.

If the U. S. Supreme Court had not created specific Miranda protections for adults, juveniles would not have received similar protections. The purpose of the Supreme Court in requiring police to advise an arrested person of his or her rights before questioning was to "police the police." The Warren Court did not trust the police or what they would do to obtain a confession and conviction. Chief Justice Earl Warren had been a strong law-and-order district attorney in Alameda County, California, where he had first-hand experience with what he could expect of over-zealous police officers, and those experiences influenced his thinking and the decisions of the Court.

The requirement to admonish an adult suspect with the *Miranda* warning has been so distorted by its use in cop shows on television and in the movies, that it is misunderstood by the general public and by some criminal justice personnel as well. Suspects usually are not *Mirandized* immediately upon arrest.

If statements from an adult suspect are to be used in trial, Miranda must be given only when two specific conditions are present at the same time:

➢ when a suspect is taken into custody, or otherwise deprived of freedom in a significant way

➢ when a suspect is subject to questioning about a crime by a police officer

These two conditions are the elements of **custodial interrogation**. Also, the adult suspect must know that the person questioning him or her is a law enforcement officer. If the suspect is not in custody, and knows that he or she is free to leave, Miranda need not be given before questioning by police. If an adult suspect is in custody but police do not question him or her, *Miranda* need not be given.

So far, the discussion of the *Miranda* procedures applies only to adults. However, the U. S. Supreme Court ruled that the procedures required by *Miranda* **apply equally to police transactions with juveniles** (*In re* **Gault, 1976**, discussed in a subsequent chapter). As far as the U.S. Supreme Court is concerned, the requirements in juvenile cases are no different than they are for adults (***Fare v. Michael C., 1979***; also see the California decision, *In re* **Bonnie H., 1997**). The "totality of the circumstances" was a guiding concept and not any possible special susceptibility of a minor.

In a decision, ***People v. Lara, 1967***, the court held that a minor has the capacity to understand his or her rights, and can knowingly and intelligently waive them, regardless of the seriousness of the alleged offense. If the minor asks to speak to a parent before responding to questions, it does not mean that the minor has invoked his or her right to remain silent.

The police officer should clarify the intent of the minor's request. If it is to ask a parent for advice about the interrogation, he or she is invoking the Fifth Amendment right to remain silent. If it is for some other purpose, to let a parent know where he or she is, for example, questioning may continue. However, the *people* (police) have the burden of proving that in requesting to see parents, the minor was not invoking his or her Fifth Amendment privilege (***People v. Burton, 1971***; also see, ***People v. Maestas, 1987***).

In a later case, ***People v. Jimenez,* 1978**, the California Supreme Court ruled that not only do the People have the burden of proving the legality of any waiver, but that it must be proven **beyond a reasonable doubt.**

In the decision, ***Fare v. Michael C., 1979***, the U. S. Supreme Court reiterated a precedent from *Lara*, the concept known as the ***totality of the circumstances*** and spelled out the factors to consider if a minor has the capacity to understand and waive his or her rights.

Case decisions have only affected the rights of minors in these situations; the parents do not have any rights, only the minor does (***In re Anthony* J., 1980**).

A decision by the U.S. Supreme Court reaffirmed this position in June 2004. Their decision arose out of the 1995 California case of Michael Alvarado, a juvenile, who was involved with friends in the murder and robbery of a truck driver in Santa Fe Springs, California. Reportedly, Alvarado had helped a friend try to steal a truck, leading to the death of the truck's owner. About one month after the killing Alvarado was called in for an interview with Los Angeles detective Cheryl Comstock. Alvarado was 17 years old at the time, and his parents brought him to the station and waited in the lobby during the interview.

Detective Comstock took Alvarado to a small room and interviewed him for approximately two hours. Alvarado was not placed under arrest, nor was he given a warning under *Miranda*. During the interview, Comstock twice asked Alvarado if he needed a break. At first, Alvarado denied being present at the shooting. Then slowly, he began to change his story, finally admitting that he had helped his friend try to steal the victim's truck and to hide the gun after the murder. When the interview was over, Comstock returned him to his parents, who drove him home.

Alvarado was arrested later on the basis of a warrant, and was charged as an adult with murder and attempted robbery. Before the trial, Alvarado's attorney moved to have Alvarado's admissions suppressed on the grounds that he had not been advised of his rights. The trial court denied his motion to suppress. The case proceeded to trial, and Alvarado was convicted in a jury trial of murder 1st and attempted robbery. The trial judge reduced the conviction to murder 2nd, and sentenced Alvarado to a term in state prison of 15 years to life. While in prison, the appellate process continued through the state and federal courts for the next nine years. Finally, on June 1, 2004 a sharply divided U. S. Supreme Court held 5 to 4 that Alvarado was not in custody for purposes of *Miranda* and his statements could be admitted at trial (***Yarborough v. Alvarado, 2004***). The conviction stood.

In J.D.B. v North Carolina (2011), a 13-year-old minor was interviewed by police officers in a room at the minor's school about bread-ins and thefts in the neighborhood. where he confessed. He was convicted, and his conviction was upheld by the North Carolina Supreme court. He was not advised of Miranda because police said that he was not in custody. However, a divided U.S. Supreme Court held that Custodial police interrogation entails "inherently compelling pressures" that risk is all the more acute when the subject of custodial interrogation is a juvenile. "So long as the child's age was known to the officer at the time of police questioning, or would have been objectively apparent to any reasonable officer, its inclusion in the custody analysis is consistent with the objective nature of the test. . ... Just as police officers are competent to account for other objective circumstances that are a matter of degree such as the length of questioning or the number of officers present, so too are they competent to evaluate the effect of relative age."

The Supreme Court reversed the judgment of the North Carolina Supreme Court and remanded the case to the lower court to determine whether, taking his age into consideration, J.D.B. was in custody when he was interrogated. "Custodial police interrogation entails "inherently compelling pressures" that risk is all the more acute when the subject of custodial interrogation is a juvenile."

California Law

Any decisions regarding *Miranda* are relevant to federal constitutional requirements. However, by using a concept known as ***independent state grounds***, a state's legislature may provide more protections than are required to satisfy the Constitution. That is what the California Legislature has done in W & I Code §625.

The §625 WIC details the procedure the officer must immediately follow in advising the minor of his or her rights.

> **In any case** where a minor is taken into temporary custody on the grounds that there is reasonable cause for believing that such a minor is a person described in Sections 601 or 602, or that he has violated an order of the juvenile court or escaped from any commitment ordered by the juvenile court, **the officer shall advise** such minor that anything he says can be used against him and shall advise him of his constitutional rights, including his right to remain silent, his right to have counsel present during any interrogation, and his right to have counsel appointed if he is unable to afford counsel.

This statute was amended by SB 395, approved by the Governor in October 2017, adding Section 625.6 to the Welfare and Institutions Code, to read:

(a) Prior to a custodial interrogation, and before the waiver of any Miranda rights, a youth 15 years of age or younger shall consult with legal counsel in person, by telephone, or by video conference. The consultation may not be waived.

§625 WIC Procedures Summarized

The cases cited above provide the guidelines for police to follow:

➤ Pursuant to §625, a minor shall **be advised** of his or her rights **in any case** when he or she is taken into temporary custody regardless of what disposition the officer might make.

➤ §625.6 requires that a minor taken into custody shall be advised of his or her right to consult with an attorney in person, by phone or by video conferencing, and cannot waive this right.

➤ If a minor gives any indication by word or conduct that he or she does not want to respond to questioning, he or she has invoked his or her Fifth Amendment privilege. Questioning must cease, and at that point police may not initiate further questioning.

➤ Police **do not** have to advise a minor of the right to speak to a parent. And, police do not have to advise the parent/s of any rights.

➤ If a minor asks to speak to a parent, the police officer may clarify the purpose and/or intent of the minor in making such a request. If it is to ask advice about responding to interrogation or to otherwise stop the questioning, the minor has invoked his or her rights. If it is about some other matter, and the minor willingly waives his or her rights, questioning may continue.

➤ A parent does not have any right to be advised that a minor is a suspect or that he or she is to be questioned, nor does the parent have the right to be present during questioning.

> In determining if the minor has the capacity to knowingly and intelligently waive his or her rights, the court will (and the police should) consider the following factors: age, intelligence, education, experience, and the ability to comprehend the meaning and effect of his or her statements. The *totality of the circumstances* is the guiding concept to bear in mind.

Miranda in Federal Juvenile Cases

Section 5033 of Title 18 of the United States Code (USC) prescribes the procedures that federal law enforcement officers must follow when taking a juvenile into custody.

Whenever a juvenile is taken into custody for an alleged act of juvenile delinquency, the arresting officer **shall immediately advise** such **juvenile** of his legal rights, in language comprehensible to a juvenile, and shall immediately notify the Attorney General **and** the juvenile's **parents**, guardian, or custodian of such custody. The arresting officer **shall also notify the parents**, guardian, or custodian of the rights of the juvenile and of the nature of the alleged offense.

Federal law, then, provides far greater protection for juveniles than is required under both Miranda and California law. This federal requirement was reaffirmed in a July 20, 2000 decision by the U.S. 9th Circuit Court of Appeals, ***U.S. v. Rudolfo R., 2000***.

Police in California might think that their procedural requirements are in compliance with some federal standard and are duplicated throughout the nation. Obviously, that is not the case. California might seem to be liberal and progressive in some aspects of its culture, but it is almost reactionary when it comes to controlling juvenile behavior.

Several other states have statutes providing juveniles with far greater protection. And, according to Cavin (1992):

> "…the scope of the additional protection afforded the juvenile ranges from an absolute requirement that an interested adult consent to the waiver to a mere

procedural requirement that parents be notified prior to questioning of the juvenile."

Interested Adult Laws

These requirements, are called **interested adult laws** because they require the advisement and/or consent of any waiver of Fifth and Sixth Amendment rights by some adult having a concern in the minor's welfare. Ohio, for example, requires consultation with an interested adult by the minor before questioning. In Indiana, legislation requires the consent of either the custodial parent, guardian, or attorney before a juvenile's rights may be waived.

In Connecticut, the Court of Appeals suppressed a juvenile's confession that was first made out of the presence of the father, and then repeated with the father present, after both the father and minor had signed a waiver. The court held that both the minor and parent should have been advised before any questioning began. Consequently, the minor's confession was tainted.

In Massachusetts, minors under the age of 14 years must consult with an interested adult before waiving any rights, while minors 14 and older must be advised and given the opportunity to consult with an interested adult. Georgia law requires merely that a minor's parents be advised upon taking a minor into custody, and allowed to consult if a request is made by the parent.

Procedures in New Hampshire follow the *totality of the circumstances*, announced in the *Lara* and *Fare* decisions. However, it has a list of fifteen factors that must be considered in determining the legality of any waiver. Georgia has a nine-factor list. North Dakota statutes and appellate decisions require that an attorney be appointed for any minor not represented by a parent or guardian, and hold that a minor absolutely cannot waive his or her rights. Only an attorney, parents or guardian can initiate a waiver.

In Oregon police must *Mirandize* a juvenile exactly as they would an adult. Police must also advise the parents before questioning the minor, and the parents or the minor may invoke the minor's Fifth and Sixth Amendment protections. However, if the minor is on probation as a ward of the court the court may waive the minor's rights (as the substitute and legal parent) and then police are not required to advise the natural parents.

Nevada seems to provide juveniles with the most protection. There police must advise the juvenile and the parent of the minor's *Miranda* rights and both must waive the rights before questioning. In addition, if the minor is of an age and has committed the type of offense that may allow for his or her waiver of jurisdiction to adult court to stand trial, police must advise him or her that anything the minor says may be used against him or her in criminal proceedings as an adult.

Fourth Amendment Protection

This constitutional guarantee is a basic right of all people regardless of age. The juvenile has the right to privacy in his or her person, automobile, and that portion of a residence normally under his or her care and control, usually a bedroom. However, as has often been the case with constitutional guarantees, it took several appellate decisions to actually create procedures to enforce that right.

The full scope of the Fourth Amendment is very broad and complex, and requires a semester-length course by itself. Here we introduce the concept of the Fourth Amendment as a framework in this section of the chapter, but then focus only on three search situations that arise out of the Exclusionary Rule.

- ➢ in-school searches of students and their effects
- ➢ police searches of probationers
- ➢ police searches of parolees

The Exclusionary Rule
In the decision of Weeks v. U.S. *1914****, the U. S. Supreme Court created what is termed the Exclusionary Rule. This is a rule of law that says*** *if evidence is seized illegally by the police, it is inadmissible in court.* **That decision was binding only on federal agents and courts, and not on local law enforcement agents. The U. S. Supreme**

Court finally made the Exclusionary Rule binding on all police agencies and courts in ***Map v. Ohio, 1961***. At that time, however, juveniles did not have any due process guarantees because of the concept of *parens patriae*, and the belief that civil procedures on behalf of juveniles without due process, were still the accepted standards. Finally, in the appellate case ***State (New Jersey) v. Lowry*, 1967**, the U. S. Supreme Court extended the Fourth Amendment protection to juveniles. (see *In re* **Scott K., 1979**).

School Searches

Minors do not have an absolute expectation of privacy in a school setting. **Administrative searches** of juveniles, their lockers, purses, or backpacks may be done only by school officials, at any time. However, any search must be based on **reasonable suspicion** that a minor has broken a school rule or violated any law, and may only be done to maintain discipline and safety on school grounds. This exception to a warrant requirement came from a case that worked its way through the New Jersey appellate process to the U. S. Supreme Court, *New Jersey v. T. L. O.* **1985**. The details are worth reviewing.

In March 1980 a fourteen-year-old high school female freshman, T.L.O. and a girlfriend were caught by a teacher smoking in a school bathroom, a violation of school rules. The teacher took the girls to the assistant vice-principal's office, where the girlfriend admitted the violation. T.L.O., however, denied the violation and claimed she did not smoke at all. The assistant vice-principal, Mr. Choplick, demanded to see T.L.O.'s purse. He opened the purse and found a pack of cigarettes, which he removed and held before T. L. O., accusing her of lying to him.

While examining the purse, Mr. Choplick also saw a pack of cigarette rolling paper, and suspected that T.L.O. might be involved in the use of marijuana. He searched the entire purse thoroughly and found some marijuana, a pipe, some empty plastic baggies, a wad of $1.00 bills, an index card listing people who owed her money, and two letters that implicated her in selling marijuana on campus. Mr. Choplick called T.L.O.'s mother and the police, and turned the evidence over to the police. At the mother's request police took T.L.O. to the police station, where she confessed to the possession and sale of marijuana at school.

Delinquency proceedings were initiated on T.L.O.'s behalf in juvenile court, where her attorney immediately moved to suppress the physical evidence and confession as fruits of an illegal search. The juvenile court denied the motion, adjudicated T.L.O a delinquent, and placed her on one year's probation. However, the defense continued the appellate process. The appellate court in New Jersey upheld the decision of the juvenile court but set aside the finding of delinquency and remanded the case back to juvenile court for a determination about whether she had knowingly and voluntarily waived her Fifth Amendment protection against self-incrimination before confessing.

T.L.O. appealed the appellate court's ruling on the Fourth Amendment search issue and the New Jersey Supreme Court reversed the decision and ordered the suppression of the evidence. Thereafter, the state appealed the case to the U.S. Supreme Court. And, after nearly five years from the date of the original incident, that Court reversed the New Jersey court's decision and stated in part that:

> requiring a teacher to obtain a warrant before searching a child suspected of an infraction of school rules (or of criminal law) would unduly interfere with the maintenance of the swift and informal disciplinary procedures needed in the schools.... We hold today that school officials need not obtain a warrant before searching a student who is under their authority.

The Court also lowered the standard of proof needed to search from the usual standard required to obtain a warrant, stating that:

> ...probable cause" is not an irreducible requirement of a valid search....The legality of a search of a student should depend simply on the reasonableness, under all the circumstances, of the search... (and)...a search of a student by a teacher or other school official will be "justified at its inception" when there are **reasonable grounds for suspecting** that the search will turn up evidence that the student has violated or is violating either the law or the rules of the school.
>
> Such a search will be permissible in its scope when the measures adopted are reasonably related to the objectives of the search and not excessively intrusive in light of the age and sex of the student and the nature of the infraction.

In its T.L.O. decision, the U.S. Supreme Court adopted the standard of **reasonable suspicion** for school searches by school officials, the same standard police must meet to detain or to patsearch someone. In addressing T.L.O.'s search, the Court found that Mr. Choplick's search was legal because the circumstances surrounding the incident created in him a reasonable suspicion that searching her purse would help prove her violation, and searching it further was based on the reasonable suspicion that she was involved in the use of marijuana.

Here, the court balanced the rights of minors with the special interests of the state and found that the interests of the State outweigh any invasion of the minor's rights, as it always has (also see, *In re* **Donaldson, 1967)**.

Any illegal activity or contraband discovered in an administrative school search may be turned over to police, and arrest and delinquency proceedings may be initiated. Police may not initiate the search but they may be called in after an administrative search, for purposes of law enforcement. Given the climate of many urban schools today police may find that they are called in on an increasing basis.

The procedural results were different in a more recent case (***Safford Unified District #1 et al. v. Redding,*** **2009** *School*). The events immediately prior to the search in question began on one October day in 2003, when the assistant principal of a middle school in Tucson, Arizona, Kerry Wilson, called 13-year-old Savana Redding from her math class at Safford Middle School. He showed Savana four white prescription-strength ibuprofen 400-mg pills, and one over-the-counter blue naproxen 200-mg pill, all used for pain and inflammation, but banned under school rules without advance permission. He asked Savana if she knew anything about the pills. Savana answered that she did not. Wilson then told Savana that he had received a report that she was giving these pills to fellow students; Savana denied it and agreed to let Wilson search her belongings. Helen Romero, an administrative assistant, came into the office, and together with Wilson they searched Savana's backpack, finding nothing.

At that point, Wilson instructed Romero to take Savana to the school nurse's office to search her clothes for pills. Romero and the nurse, Peggy Schwallier, asked Savana to remove her jacket, socks, and shoes, leaving her in stretch pants and a T-shirt (both without pockets), which she was then asked to remove. Finally, Savana was told to pull her bra out and to the side and shake it, and to pull out the elastic on her underpants, thus exposing her breasts and pelvic area to some degree. No pills were found.

The young girl's parents filed suit, claiming an invasion of privacy by school officials, in violation of the Fourth Amendment. The case dragged on through a lengthy appellate process of nearly six years. Finally, the U. S. Supreme Court rendered a decision in June 2009. According to the justices:

> The issue here is whether a 13-year-old student's Fourth Amendment right was violated when she was subjected to a search of her bra and underpants by school officials acting on reasonable suspicion that she had brought forbidden prescription and over-the-counter drugs to school. Because there were no reasons to suspect the drugs presented a danger or were concealed in her underwear, we hold that the search did violate the Constitution. ...

In this case, the court balanced the rights of the minor with the special interests of the state and found that the interests of the minor and the intrusiveness of the search outweighed any special interests of the state. The search was not reasonable and was too intrusive vis-à-vis any danger to the public safety.

Police Searches of Probationers

Probationers were always treated with a combination of helping the minor and enforcing the probation conditions. Today, however, juveniles on probation are more sophisticated, more prone to violence, more independent of parental controls and values, more gang oriented, and more fatalistic in their views of what life has to offer them, compared to their counterparts of twenty (or even ten) years ago. These changes have brought a shift in the views of probation officers to add a stronger enforcement dimension to their casework supervision. Many departments now have special supervision units in which the probation officers might be armed.

This change in delinquent behavior has also stimulated probation, parole, and the courts to make increasing use of controlling strategies to facilitate supervision in the community. One primary strategy is known as the **3-way search clause**, a condition of probation that requires probationers to waive their Fourth Amendment protection against warrantless searches.

The wording of these clauses, or conditions, may vary from county to county, but the condition usually **requires the minor to submit his or her person, automobile, or place of residence to search and seizure by any peace officer, without a warrant**.

What began as an enforcement tool in probation narcotics cases in the 1960s is now used in most every type of case to control the varieties of delinquent conduct. What once was the prerogative of probation officers in supervising their wards is now a basic tactic of law enforcement, especially in gang suppression operations.

As one might imagine, requiring a person to waive his or her Fourth Amendment protection has not gone unchallenged by defense attorneys seeking to represent their clients against new charges and/or supervision violations. These defense appeals have been useful in that the appellate decisions have established the procedural guidance for police in searching probationers, and have distinguished what is a reasonable expectation of privacy for probationers in contrast to parolees.

Selected cases are presented below within the context of the enforcement situations that gave rise to the appeals against police practices so that the reader can appreciate just what the ground rules are for police searches.

Over the years, police officers have used the search condition imposed on a minor's probation as a way to manage delinquent behavior that they encounter on the street. Officers could stop and search any minor on probation, or his or her vehicle, or that part of the residence under the care and control of the minor. Enforcement actions, however, were challenged in a number of appellate decisions over the issue of what rights to privacy were retained by a minor and whether officers could justify an illegal search after the fact, when it was learned that the minor was on probation at the time, but the officer did not know that. Appellate decisions varied as well, and often held that: a minor's rights may be legitimately restricted to serve the state's interest in promoting the health and welfare of juveniles. At one point, the California Supreme Court held that evidence found in what could be described as a *dirty* search would be legal if officers later learned that the minor was on probation with a search clause (***In re* Tyrell, J., 1994**).

Finally, in November 2006, the California Supreme Court did a complete reversal on a portion of its previous *Tyrell* decision and **held that a peace officer must have prior knowledge of the search clause and its scope in advance of any search. (*In re* Jaime P., 2006)**. The Court concluded that:

➢ The probationer has no standing to object to any search order.

➢ Searches may not exceed the scope of the consent, as worded in the condition imposed.

➢ A search of a probationer may be conducted only for reasons related to the rehabilitative and reformative purposes of probation or for any other legitimate law enforcement purpose.

➢ Searches may not be undertaken for harassment or for arbitrary or capricious reasons.

➢ Before a police officer may search a juvenile based solely on a probation search clause, the officer **must have prior knowledge of the search clause** and its scope, and the search may not exceed that scope.

Parole Searches

There have been very few appellate decisions about juvenile parole searches. The following case about an adult parolee helped to establish some sort of precedent. (***Pennsylvania Board of Probation and Parole v. Scott, 1998***). In the *Scott* case, the U.S. Supreme Court held that the exclusionary rule does not apply in parole searches. In effect, this decision removed all Fourth Amendment protections for parolees. This opened the door for states to enact laws allowing parole searches without requiring any cause. An exception to allowing parole searches on demand, however, was articulated in the juvenile parolee search case, ***In re* Michael T., 1993**. It placed a qualification on the knowledge that police need to have before initiating any search. The 5th DCA held that a search of a CYA parolee by police who have no knowledge of the search clause is invalid unless the officer's conduct is "reasonable under the ordinary Fourth Amendment standard."

The California Supreme Court has followed this same line of thinking in a more recent parolee search decision (***People v. Sanders, 2003***), which held that a police search of a parolee is invalid unless the police have prior knowledge of the parolee's status and search clause.

It would seem that in both probation searches and parole searches the police must have prior knowledge of a parolee's status and the scope of the search clause before effecting any search.

Juvenile Gangs: Control and Suppression

When juvenile gangs first came to public prominence, they were usually associated with inner-city neighborhoods and large urban centers in major cities such as New York, Los Angeles, or Chicago. However, today the prevalence of juvenile gangs and gang violence is alarming and it is everywhere. Once an urban problem, street gangs have now infiltrated communities large and small throughout the United States

Long-established domestic gangs like the Bloods and the Crips remain powerful, but the problem has worsened dramatically in recent years. Heavy immigration, particularly from Latin America and Asia, has introduced highly violent gangs like Mara Salvatrucha and the Almighty Latin Kings Nation. Bound by tight ethnic and racial ties, they often stymie police investigations by assaulting or killing potential witnesses. Having already diversified from illegal drugs into auto theft, extortion, property crimes and home invasion, some East Coast gangs have begun trafficking in fraudulent identification papers that could be used by terrorists.

In California gangs are obviously more concentrated in larger cities such as Los Angeles, Oakland, and San Francisco, but they are also very active in the Bakersfield area, in the Sacramento Valley, in the San Joaquin Valley, and in almost every city, town, village, and county one can name. One must deliberately seek out a remote section of California, far from primary transportation routes, and the madding crowd, to be free from the threat posed by street gangs. Today however, one might find that gangs have formed there too.

Gang Formations and Activities

Gangs often form among the youth of economically and/or socially disadvantaged families living in the poorer areas of a community. Frequently there is only one parent in the home. Gangs also seem to cluster along the major transportation corridors throughout the state in order to create favorable drug distribution networks.

One of the primary activities of some street gangs is drug sales, and much of the violence between gangs is over the control of drug distribution.

Gangs fight each other over territory as well. For example, there has been an on-going war for years between the Hispanics from the north and those from the south, with Bakersfield as the dividing line. This started over 40 years ago in Folsom Prison by two Hispanics arguing over the ownership of a pair of shoes. As a result, many individuals have died over the past years because the memberships of these two gangs are sworn mortal enemies. To add to these two dominant Hispanic gangs, the Sureños and Norteños, we now have the Sinaloan Cowboys.

We also have a new gang phenomenon, the hybrid gangs. These tend to be diverse in race, ethnicity, and gender. They are often formed by traditional gang members who relocate and need to join or form other associations, and blend with other non-traditional groups. They might also represent a coalition formed to control some sort of criminal activity in a given area, such as drug trade.

Gangs have expanded their repertoire of crimes, as well, to broaden the threat they pose to the general community. Some gangs, particularly certain Asian gangs, specialize in extortion and home invasion robbery. The victims are often Asians themselves, many of whom do not trust the American institutions such as banks and police. Other gangs specialize in carjacking and still others in party crash robbery. This latter crime is increasing among juveniles. Twelve to fifteen youths will crash a house party given by another juvenile while the parents are away and steal everything that is not nailed down.

The initiation of a new gang member, or ***jumping-in***, as it is called, poses an equally serious threat. A young boy wanting to join a gang might have to rob, assault, or shoot someone, just to prove his or her mettle. A young girl might have to steal or give herself sexually to the other gang members in order to gain gang acceptance. If a gang accepts girl members but is run by boys, the ***jumping-in*** will almost always include sexual favors for the boys. There is an alarming increase in girl gangs, dominated primarily by Caucasian girls. Their *jumping-in* process often includes having the prospective member fight four or five gang members for two minutes without falling down or giving up.

Why Juveniles Join Gangs

Juveniles join gangs for a number of reasons. For those who live in urban areas of large cities, it could be for protection and safety. A juvenile alone can be assaulted or killed on the street just for what he wears, or just for being there. There is strength in numbers and, for some juveniles, survival from day to day depends on the strength of their gang.

Once gangs form and engage in criminal activity, the profits from drug sales, burglaries, and robberies provide a motivation to remain a member. The fun and camaraderie the members experience together is also a deciding factor for remaining in a gang. Also, it is the one place they are accepted, and often loved, without qualifications or conditions; something many of their families do not do.

In some cultural groupings, primarily in urban centers, gang affiliation has become a way of life. One becomes a member of a certain gang by virtue of the street on which his parents live. He does not know any other way, and if he does, few alternatives are available to live otherwise. Gangs can also be generational. It is not uncommon to find all the males of one family in the same gang, with the father in or just out of prison, the older brother on parole from the Youth Authority for the third time, and young junior on his way to court for his first assault.

Finally, juveniles join gangs because the affiliation gives meaning to their otherwise empty lives. It becomes an extended family from which they can receive acceptance, self-esteem, security, power, and friendship from shared experiences. They also feel independent and free from parental control. The members become bonded to each other while they are rejected by the mainstream of society.

California's Legal Definition of a Street Gang

In some of the large urban centers, the police have become an occupation force on foreign soil, too small in numbers to really keep the peace. The gangs are beyond control, and the police can do no more than react to a growing array of crimes. It will take something just short of an all-out-war to win back certain communities. Certainly, law enforcement cannot do it alone. Community leaders from all walks of life and parents must assume a substantial amount of responsibility in providing alternatives to gang activities for their youth.

The primary responsibility of the police is the detection, control, and suppression of street gang crime and violence. To aid the police in their efforts, in 1988, the Legislature enacted Penal Code Section 186.22, known as the **Street Terrorism Enforcement and Prevention (STEP) Act**. The Legislature declared California to be:

> ...in a state of crisis which has been caused by violent street gangs whose members threaten, terrorize, and commit a multitude of crimes against the peaceful citizens of their neighborhoods. These activities, both individually and collectively, present a clear and present danger to public order and safety and are not constitutionally protected.

Penal Code Section 186.22 (f) defines a **criminal street gang** as:
...the ongoing organization, association, or group of three or more persons, whether formal or informal having as one of its primary activities the commission of one or more of the criminal acts (25 are listed in the code)...which has a common name or identifying sign or symbol, whose members individually or collectively engage in or have engaged in a pattern of criminal gang activity.

The original legislation listed 21 violent and serious felonies that came to be known as *gang crimes*. Proposition 21, passed by the California voters on March 7, 2000, added additional crimes to the list, as well as additional enhancements (additional institutional time) that related to the offender's background and the nature of the offense.

Punishment for Street Gang Offenses

The law is complicated, and it has two parts. Penal Code Section 186.22 (a) makes it a crime to actively participate in a gang under the following circumstances:

- With knowledge that its members engage/engaged in a pattern of criminal activity, and
- Willfully promote, further, or assist felonious conduct by the gang members.

The courts define "active participation" as taking part in gang activity. One does not have to be a member of the gang, or a leader of the gang; one can be an associate. One knows that the gang you associate with commits or has committed more than one crime, and you willfully help the gang by either committing a crime, or aiding and abetting a crime.

Penal Code Section 186.22(b) provides a sentence enhancement for committing a felony crime for the benefit of, at the direction of, or in association with a criminal street gang. The institutional commitment time of a juvenile may be enhanced (increased) in the same manner as adult sentences. If the prosecution alleges in a juvenile court petition that their clothes, colors, tattoos, and their graffiti writings. If the minor committed a gang offense, as a gang member, the CYA commitment time may be enhanced by 16 months, 2 years, or 3 years.

If the offense is a serious felony, as defined in subdivision (c) of §1192.7 PC, and is committed on the grounds of, or within 1,000 feet of, a public or private elementary, vocational,

junior high, or high school, during school hours in which the facility is open for classes or school-related programs or when minors are using the facility, the court may enhance the offense by a term of 2, 3, or 4 years, at the judge's discretion.

Under §186.22(i) PC:
> In order to...sustain a juvenile petition, pursuant to subdivision (a), it is not necessary for the prosecution to prove that the person devotes all, or a substantial part of his or her time or efforts to the criminal street gang, nor is it necessary to prove that the person is a member of the criminal street gang. **Active participation in the criminal street gang is all that is required.**

Street Gang Registration Requirements

Effective March 8, 2000, with the passage of Proposition 21 (§186.30 PC) any minor adjudicated in juvenile court for any gang offense is required to register with the chief of police of the city in which he or she resides, or the sheriff of the county if he or she resides in an unincorporated area, within 10 days of release from custody or within 10 days of his or her arrival in any city or county.

The registration process is detailed in §186.32 PC, and it is very comprehensive. The minor must appear at the appropriate law enforcement agency with his or her parent or guardian, complete the required forms, and submit to fingerprinting and photographing.

At any time that the minor changes his or her address, he or she must notify the registering law enforcement agency within ten days. If the move is to a new police jurisdiction, the minor must reregister with the new agency and advise the previous agency of the move within ten days. Failure to register will be treated as a misdemeanor for court purposes. However, if the minor fails to register and commits a new gang offense, an enhancement of 16 months, 2 years, or 3 years may be added to any commitment time.

Police Gang Suppression

In many law enforcement agencies, officers are assigned to a gang control or suppression unit or to a county **task force**, as previously mentioned. Frequently these officers are detectives who specialize in investigating and suppressing gang related offenses.

A primary element of police street gang suppression tactics is the identification of gangs and gang members, and the tracking of their movements and activities. Gang members can be identified by graffiti. Graffiti is the language of the street, and identifies gang territories, gang members, and challenges to or from other gangs.

Another element in the police officer's suppression efforts is to document who the gang members are, then hand deliver a documentation letter from the local district attorney to the gang member, making him or her eligible for offense enhancements and punishment.

The criteria for documentation are:

- the minor admits membership
- is identified by a reliable informant
- appears in gang photos or documents
- is identified by another known gang member
- is identified by an untested informant plus corroboration by independent information

> is taken into custody with known gang members in the commission of an offense

On June 6, 2006 Attorney General Alberto R. Gonzales **announced** that the U.S. Department of Justice (DOJ) is distributing nearly $15 million in **grant funds** through the **Gang Resistance Education And Training (G.R.E.A.T.) Program**. Administered by the **Office of Justice Programs'** (OJP's) **Bureau of Justice Assistance**, the program seeks to reduce the involvement of elementary and middle school students in delinquent behavior, violence, and gangs through its classroom curriculum, taught by law enforcement officers.

Task or Strike Force Organizations

In many urban areas juvenile activities are not limited to specific areas nor are they limited to the traditional delinquent offenses. Violent offenses by juveniles are up 30 percent, and rising. Gang involvement accounts for most of this increase, and the use of guns by juveniles is commonplace. Consequently, many police agencies are combining resources to form task forces to suppress gang activities that often are county-wide or region-wide. For example, on June 25, 2004, 85 officers from nearly a dozen law enforcement agencies, including local police, county sheriff's deputies, the FBI, and CHP, conducted a three-county anti-gang sweep in the northern California counties of Butte, Glenn, and Sutter. They made arrests and confiscated illegal guns.

Often task forces include probation officers and parole agents, because many gang members are either on probation or parole, giving the suppression efforts more scope. With the passage of Proposition 21, it has become easier to identify and track gang members because of the registration process, and it has facilitated the use of the task force approach to gang suppression.

Summary

In the first portion of the chapter we have seen that the federal case law (*Miranda*) requires that police advise a suspect of his or her Fifth Amendment right to remain silent and Sixth Amendment right to an attorney before custodial interrogation may begin. In

California, however, Section 625 WIC requires police to advise a minor of those rights *in any case* after a minor has been taken into temporary custody.

We have detailed the fact that a minor has the capacity to understand and waive those rights, depending upon the *totality of the circumstances*. Parents have no rights at all under §625. It was noted that by the concept known as *independent state grounds*, a state may provide greater legal protection to a suspect or minor than the minimum required by the Constitution. The requirements under §625 to advise a minor "…in any case…", is an example of that, as are all the *interested adult laws* cited. However, the adherent to that requirement, apart from a Miranda warning, receives little attention from police or the courts.

Next, we examined the Fourth Amendment protection against unreasonable search and seizure and how that full protection is denied juveniles in certain situations: administrative searches by school officials, and police searches of probationers and parolees. Probation and parole conditions usually include a 3-way search clause. Finally, we discussed the juvenile gang phenomena, why juveniles join gangs, and the application of street gang laws designed to suppress gang activity. We concluded this chapter with a discussion of street gangs and the laws and punishments for gang activities by minors. It was suggested that a systems approach, such as a task force, including probation, parole, and police, would be the most effective way to approach street gang suppression.

References

Cavin, Jeffrey D. "Waiver of a Juvenile's Fifth and Sixth Amendment Rights," Journal *of Juvenile Justice*, Vol. 13, 1992, pp. 27-41

Case Decisions

Fare v. Michael C. (1979) 442 U.S. 707

In re Anthony J. (1980) 107 CA 3rd 962

In re Bonnie H. (1997) 56 CA 4th 563

In re Donaldson (1967) 209 CA 2d 509

In re Gault (1976) 37 U. S. 1

In re Michael T., (2003) 14 CA 4th 1151

In re Scott K. (1979) 24 C 3d 395; 155 Cal. Rptr. 671

In re Tyrell J. (1994) 8 CA 4th 68

J.D.B. v. North Carolina, 131 S. Ct. 2394, 2397

Mapp v. Ohio (1961) 367 U. S. 643

Miranda v. Arizona (1966) 384 U. S. 436

New Jersey v. T.L.O. (1985) 469 U. S. 325

Pennsylvania Board of Probation and Parole v. Scott, 524 U.S. 357 (1998)

People v. Burton (1971) 6 Cal. 3d 375

People v. Jimenez (1978) 21 CA 3d 595

People v. Lara (1967) 62 Cal. 586

People v. Maestas (1987) 194 CA 3rd 1499

People v. Sanders, (2003) Ct.App. 5 F033862

Safford Unified School District #1 et al. v. Redding. (2009)   No. 08-479

State (New Jersey) v. Lowry, 1967

U.S. v. Rudolfo (2000) No. 99-50250

Weeks v. U. S. (1914) 232 U.S. 383

Yarborough v. Alvarado, 541 US. 652

Chapter 6: Juvenile Due Process and Jurisdiction Waiver Procedures

Key Terms and Concepts

Adjudication
Direct filing
Double jeopardy
Due process
Fifth Amendment
Fitness criteria
Fitness Hearing
Fitness Report
Fourteenth Amendment

Judicial finding
Judicial waiver
Legislative waiver
Preponderance of evidence
Presumption of fitness
Proof beyond a reasonable doubt
Self-incrimination
Sixth Amendment
Special fitness categories
Waiver of jurisdiction

Introduction

The chapter on the history of the juvenile justice system described the early philosophy of the court as one of protection. Juveniles, who could not care for themselves, who became wayward, or who violated the law, needed the court to intervene as a benevolent parent.

This philosophy originated early in the development of juvenile law and procedures and it was the pervasive line of thinking in California and throughout the United States until 1966. Juveniles did not need constitutional protections and due process because the court intervened on their behalf. If they were removed from the custody of their parents and placed in an institutional setting, it was for their own good. They were to receive training and treatment to make them better people. In his book, Anthony Platt accurately describes this era as the "child saver period" (1969). The court was duty-bound to save them, even if it destroyed them in the process.

Beginning in 1966, the U. S. Supreme Court reviewed a series of juvenile cases on appeal and, in almost exposé fashion, criticized the juvenile courts for acting contrary to this benevolent philosophy. In fact, the Court found that far too often the juvenile was denied both protection and due process. In response to these abuses, the Court extended the protections of the Fourteenth Amendment to juvenile proceedings and guaranteed juveniles the Fifth Amendment privilege against self-incrimination and all the Sixth Amendment privileges except the right to a public trial and a jury trial.

In the first portion of this chapter, five of these appellate cases are reviewed, beginning with the *Kent* decision, so that the reader can appreciate the Court's reasoning behind the procedures mandated.

As it is with most case law these decisions were in response to flagrant abuses of individual rights by the system. However, these abuses were the norm, not the exception.

The second portion of the chapter details the original fitness hearing and jurisdictional waiver procedures that were required by the *Kent* decision, then examines the additional waiver procedures provided by Proposition 21, enacted in 2000.

Juvenile Due Process Case

Kent v. U. S., 1966

A procedure known as the **Fitness Hearing** was mentioned earlier in this book, but no details were given. Basically, it was a hearing to determine whether a minor is fit to remain in juvenile court and receive rehabilitative treatment. A minor found unfit, was certified to adult court to stand trial under criminal proceedings, with all the constitutional protections of any other adult. The district attorney (state) was the only one who can initiate this hearing.

These fitness hearings were once very informal, with no due process, and no particular procedures. Then along came Morris Kent, a young resident of Washington D. C. In 1959, at age 14, Kent was adjudicated a delinquent for attempting to steal a woman's purse and for breaking into several houses. He was placed on probation in the physical custody of his mother, and he was seen regularly by his probation officer over the next two years. During this period of supervision, the probation officer compiled a file that reflected how Kent responded to probation.

On September 2, 1961, someone entered a woman's apartment in the city, raped her, and left with her wallet. Fingerprints found at the scene matched those of Kent taken at the time of his first arrest two years earlier. He was taken into custody by police and interrogated, and he confessed to the offenses. He also confessed to committing several other similar break-ins, robberies, and rapes.

States vary in the age at which a juvenile can be found unfit and then can transfer jurisdiction to adult court. In Washington D. C., it was age 16. A petition was filed on behalf of Kent in juvenile court alleging three counts each of housebreaking and robbery, and two counts of rape. His mother retained an attorney who had Kent examined by two psychiatrists. They diagnosed Kent as suffering from severe psychopathology and in need of hospitalization. They recommended that he remain under the jurisdiction of the juvenile court and receive treatment.

The probation officer recommended that the court waive jurisdiction and transfer the case to adult court. The judge followed this recommendation and, without any hearing, certified Morris Kent to adult court. Kent was immediately indicted by the grand jury on all counts. In his first trial, he was tried on the rape charges and found not guilty by reason of insanity. In a second trial, he was tried and found guilty on the break-ins and robbery charges, and was sentenced to six consecutive terms of 5 to 15 years in prison.

If Morris Kent had been found fit as a juvenile, he could have remained under the court's jurisdiction (probably in an institution) until his 21st birthday; six years maximum. Instead, he received an adult sentence that could run 90 years. The disparity is obvious.

On appeal, the U. S. Supreme Court found that the juvenile court judge had waived jurisdiction without conducting a full investigation, without a hearing, without recording any reason as to why Kent was unfit, without actually making a legal finding as to unfitness, and without allowing Kent's attorney access to the probation file that contained the information used by the judge in his decision. This was a serious abuse of judicial discretion.

In 1966 the Supreme Court reversed Kent's convictions and established the following procedures that must be followed in any fitness, or waiver of jurisdiction hearing:

- a full investigation must be conducted of all the issues concerning fitness
- there must be a hearing with the minor present
- the minor has the right to an attorney to represent him or her at this hearing
- the attorney has the right to discovery
- the judge must state on the record the reason/s for waiving jurisdiction

The real significance of the Kent decision was that for the first-time **due process became a part of juvenile court proceedings**.

In re Gault, 1967

On June 8, 1964, a 15-year-old Arizona boy named Gerald Gault, and his friend Ronald Lewis, were taken into custody by the Gila County Sheriff on a complaint from a Mrs. Cook that they had made obscene phone calls to her. They were taken immediately to the local detention facility. Gault's parents were at work, and were not informed of his arrest or detention.

Gault was on probation at the time, and his probation officer arranged for a delinquency hearing for the following day. His parents were not advised of the hearing until that morning. Neither Gault nor his parents were informed of the specific charges. They were not advised of any constitutional rights. The so-called victim, Mrs. Cook, did not appear in court to give evidence.

The probation officer provided hearsay information to the judge as to what she alleged Gerald had said. The petition was filed by the probation officer at the hearing, but it did not cite the specific allegation. The wording stated that "…said minor is under the age of 18 years and is in need of protection of this Honorable Court…(and that)… said minor is a delinquent…."

The case was continued for a week to allow time for a report from the probation officer. Gault's mother requested that Mrs. Cook come to court and identify who had made the phone calls, but the judge said her presence was not necessary. On June 15, 1964, Judge McGee found Gerald Gault delinquent for making "lewd phone calls," and committed him to the Arizona Industrial School until his 21st birthday, or until paroled.

If he had been convicted as an adult, Gault could have been fined a maximum of $50 or jailed for 60 days. Instead, he was deprived of his freedom for up to six years, without any due process for making three phone calls to Mrs. Cook in which he said: "Are your cherries ripe? Are you giving any away today? Do you have big bombers?"

An attorney was retained to appeal the case, but he was frustrated to find that Arizona law did not provide for appellate review of juvenile cases. Finally, after considerable legal effort, the case was accepted on a Writ of *Certiorari* by the U. S. Supreme Court. In May 1967, the Court reversed Gault's conviction and mandated that the Fifth Amendment privilege against self-incrimination and most of the Sixth Amendment be applied to any juvenile court hearing in which the consequence could be the loss of freedom; this refers to any adjudication hearing (trial).

The Gault decision extended the *Miranda* warning to juvenile procedures, beginning with police contact. In addition, a minor was guaranteed the right to notice of the charges, to an attorney, to cross examine witnesses, to present witnesses, and the protection against self- incrimination. The only Sixth Amendment rights not given to juveniles were a public trial and a jury trial by one's peers. The Supreme Court Justices hoped that by their decision, juveniles would receive the best of both worlds: the constitutional protections accorded an adult and the *parens patriae protection* of a benevolent juvenile court.

In re Winship, 1970

Sam Winship, a 12-year-old New York boy was taken into custody by police for breaking into a locker and stealing $112 from a woman's purse. Juvenile court proceedings were initiated on his behalf; he was adjudicated a delinquent; and he was committed to a reform school for 18 months, with a provision that the commitment could be extended until Winship's 18th birthday.

The New York juvenile court proceedings were civil, not criminal (just as it is now in California). Consequently, the standard of proof used in civil cases also applied. This standard is the **preponderance of the evidence**, which means a probability of guilt, not a certainty. In Winship's case, the judge acknowledged that he had some doubts as to his guilt. Nevertheless, he "probably" did the act, and was deprived of his freedom for what could amount to six years. The case was appealed.

The standard of proof required in criminal cases has been proof beyond a reasonable doubt since 1798. In the *Winship* case, the U. S. Supreme Court wanted to preserve the civil and protective nature of juvenile court, but it also wanted to uphold a basic principle of American law, innocent until and unless proven guilty. The Court reversed his adjudication as a delinquent and his case was dismissed. Of course, by then he had already served the eighteen months.

In its decision, the Court held that:

> ...the Due Process clause (of the Fourteenth Amendment) protects the accused against conviction except upon proof beyond a reasonable doubt of every fact necessary to constitute the crime with which he is charged.

The Supreme Court mandated that the standard of **proof beyond a reasonable doubt** shall apply in any juvenile proceeding in which it is alleged that a juvenile committed an act that would be a crime if committed by an adult. In California, this means any §602 adjudication hearing (trial). (See, *In re* **Steven C., 1970**, California's first case).

McKeiver v. Pennsylvania, 1971

In May 1968, Joseph McKeiver, age 16, was charged with robbery, larceny, and receiving stolen property, all felonies. His attorney requested a jury trial, but it was denied, and he was adjudicated a delinquent. His appeal that he had been denied the Sixth Amendment right to a jury trial was not upheld by the Pennsylvania Supreme Court.

In a similar case in January 1969, Edward Terry, age 15, was charged with assault and battery on a police officer, and conspiracy. His attorney also requested a jury trial, but it was denied, and Terry was adjudicated a delinquent. On appeal, his conviction was also affirmed by the Pennsylvania Supreme Court. Both the McKeiver and Terry cases were consolidated in 1971 on appeal to the U. S. Supreme Court on the narrow question of whether the Sixth Amendment right to a jury trial applied to juvenile court proceedings. The Court did not want to weaken the informality and civil nature of juvenile proceedings any more than it already had under *Gault* and *Winship*. The Court first referred to a principle enunciated in a 1968 adult case, *Duncan v. Louisiana* "...that trial by jury in criminal cases is fundamental to the American scheme of justice."

The Court went on to say that a juvenile court proceeding "...has **not yet been held to be a criminal prosecution** within the meaning of the Sixth Amendment..." The Court affirmed the convictions of McKeiver and Terry and held **that juveniles were not constitutionally entitled to a jury trial** because proceedings were still civil, not criminal. A state may enact its own legislation that provides a jury in juvenile proceedings, but it is not required to do so. The California Supreme Court has continued to rule that juveniles do not have a right to a jury trial (*In re* **Steven C, 1970**, *In re* **Roger S., 1977**, and *In re* **Scott K., 1979**).

Breed v. Jones, 1975

This case originated in Los Angeles on February 9, 1971, when a 602 petition was filed on behalf of Gary Steven Jones, a 17 year old boy, alleging armed robbery. Court proceedings began in the typical manner with an adjudication hearing on March 1, during which witnesses and other evidence were presented. At the conclusion of the hearing, the court found the allegations to be true, sustained the petition, and continued the case to March 15 for the dispositional hearing (sentencing). The case was referred to a probation officer to complete an investigation and report on Jones, including a recommendation and a treatment plan.

The court opened the dispositional hearing on March 15 by stating that its intention was to waive jurisdiction and certify Jones to adult court to stand trial for a crime. The defense counsel was taken by surprise and immediately moved for a continuance. The case was put over for one week. When the second hearing opened, the judge stated that he had read and considered the report of the probation officer. Then, he listened to the mother's comments, after which he declared Jones unfit to remain in juvenile court and waived jurisdiction.

Jones was ordered to stand trial in adult court, and a complaint was filed against him charging one count of armed robbery. The defense attorney petitioned the juvenile court on a Writ of *Habeas Corpus*, claiming that Jones had been placed in double jeopardy. The petition was denied. Counsel appealed to the Court of Appeals, Second District, but was denied. He then appealed to the State Supreme Court, which refused to hear the case (***In re* Gary Steven J., 1971**).

Meanwhile, in adult court, Jones was held to answer for trial at the preliminary hearing. By stipulation, the matter was submitted to the trial court on the transcript of the preliminary hearing. The judge found Jones guilty of 1st degree robbery. Rather than sentence Jones as an adult, the judge suspended criminal proceedings and committed him to the California Youth Authority where he could remain until age 25. This is a procedure often used when a judge finds an adult between the ages of 18 and 21 too immature to warrant a prison sentence.

On December 10, 1971, Jones' mother, acting as his guardian filed a Writ of *Habeas Corpus* in the U. S. District Court, claiming double jeopardy. That court denied her petition. However, the District Court of Appeals reversed the lower court's decision and held that Jones was placed in double jeopardy when he was made to stand trial in adult court after already having been adjudicated in juvenile court. The State appealed to the U. S. Supreme Court.

Finally, in 1975, the U. S. Supreme Court agreed with the Court of Appeals and held that the **double jeopardy clause of the Fifth Amendment applies in juvenile proceedings**. If a juvenile court wants to waive jurisdiction, it must do so before the adjudication hearing. Once the adjudication hearing begins, **jeopardy attaches** to the minor, and he or she may not be "re-tried."

Of course, by this time Jones had already completed his treatment (served time) at CYA, and was beyond the jurisdiction of the juvenile court. (Breed was named in the Writ because Breed was Director of the California Youth Authority at the time, and a Writ of *Habeas Corpus* names the person who has custody of the petitioner).

Jurisdiction Waiver Procedures

This chapter began with a review of the *Kent* decision in which the U. S. Supreme Court detailed the procedures that must be followed to waive jurisdiction of a juvenile case to adult court. The *Kent* was to give juveniles the due process they had been denied. Section 707 WIC provides for these mandated procedures, as well as for the detailed criteria used to assess the fitness of a juvenile.

Section 707 has been amended from time to time, first to lower the age of whom may be found unfit from 16 to 14 years, then secondly, to allow direct prosecution in certain limited cases. Proposition 21 was enacted to provide additional opportunities for direct prosecution in criminal court.

Prior to March 8, 2000, the effective date of Proposition 21, the WIC provided two procedures in which minors could be prosecuted as adults. First, if a minor age 16 or over faced allegations of serious felonies listed in §602(b), and had one or more prior adjudications (the juvenile equivalent of an adult conviction), the matter could be filed directly in adult court. The second procedure allowed the district attorney to file a motion in juvenile court requesting the court to find the minor "unfit" for juvenile proceedings. This required a fitness hearing, as provided for in *Kent*.

Proposition 21 created **two additional methods, for a total of three,** by which juvenile court jurisdiction over a minor may be waived and the minor prosecuted as an adult. These may be characterized (see Datig) as:

➢ the **legislative waiver**, in which the juvenile court has no jurisdiction over certain offenses committed by (today) minors age 16 or older (Modified, as described below).

➢ **direct filing**, in which the prosecutor has the discretion to by-pass juvenile court and file certain cases in adult criminal court   No longer allowed, as of 2018.

➢ **judicial waiver**, which uses a fitness hearing procedure in juvenile court as mandated by *Kent*.

We will first discuss the judicial waiver and fitness hearing procedures, followed by an examination of the other two waiver methods that were created by Proposition 21 and Proposition 57.

Senate Bill 1391

Before we take up any discussion of these waiver procedures, we address the most recent legislative changes. In 2016, the voters of California approved Proposition 57 which provided specific procedures for the waiver of jurisdiction from juvenile court to criminal court for youth ages 14 and 15 years. The justification believed at the time was that those youths were sufficiently mature to be held accountable for certain listed crimes, as adults. That thinking was also reflected in legislation of the 1990s that provided procedures for transferring jurisdiction of youths ages 14 years and over to criminal court. That thinking changed over the next two years and the legislature enacted new procedures in the form of Senate Bill 1391.

Senate Bill (SB) 1391, is one of the most significant acts to modify juvenile procedures in many years. It represents a reversal in defining the age of responsibility for juveniles. It amends Section 707 of the Welfare and Institutions Code relating to juveniles defining the age at which a juvenile may be tried as an adult.

Prior to the approval of **SB 1391** by Governor Brown in August 2018, existing law enacted by Proposition 57 allowed the district attorney to make a motion to transfer a minor from juvenile court to a court of criminal jurisdiction in a case in which a minor is alleged to have committed a felony when he or she was 16 years of age or older **or** in a case in which a specified serious offenses is alleged to have been committed by a minor **when he or she was 14 or 15 years of age**.

SB 1391 modifies §707 WIC and repeals the authority of a district attorney to make a motion to transfer a minor from juvenile court to a court of criminal jurisdiction as it relates to **14 and 15-year-olds**. By increasing the number of minors retained under the jurisdiction of the juvenile court, this bill also imposes state-mandated local programs. The California Constitution requires the state to reimburse local agencies and school districts for certain costs mandated by the state, such as rehabilitation programs.

Under SB 1391, all 14-year-olds and 15-year-olds charged with any offense must be handled in the juvenile justice system. Under no circumstances would anyone younger than age 16 be tried in adult court, even on homicide charges.

According to supporters of the bill, "Cognitive science has proven that children and youth who commit crimes are very capable of change," said State Senator Ricardo Lara (D), the bill's author, in an interview this summer with *The Chronicle of Social Change*. "Sending youth to an adult prison does not help our youth and does not make our communities any safer."

In California, youths who are incarcerated following an adult conviction are placed in a juvenile facility until they are mature adults. Supporters of SB 1391 argue that keeping 14 and 15-year-old offenders in the juvenile justice system will reduce recidivism rates and better rehabilitate and prepare youth for successful, productive re-entry into society. That might well be the case.

However, as an example of the effect this change might have, consider an extreme situation in which two juvenile friends commit a homicide. One is age 16 and one is age 15. The 16-year-old gets convicted in adult court and is sentenced to prison, but because of his tender age, he is placed in a youth institution. The 15-year-old is adjudicated through juvenile court and found to have committed the offense and is considered to be a danger to the community, so he is committed to a youth facility, where he might bunk with his 16-year-old friend.

The complete Section 707 WIC is given below for the reader's edification.

THE PEOPLE OF THE STATE OF CALIFORNIA DO ENACT AS FOLLOWS:

SECTION 1.
Section 707 of the Welfare and Institutions Code is amended to read:
707.
(a) (1) In any case in which a minor is alleged to be a person described in Section 602 by reason of the violation, when he or she was 16 years of age or older, of any offense listed in subdivision (b) or any other felony criminal statute, the district attorney or other appropriate prosecuting officer may make a motion to transfer the minor from juvenile court to a court of criminal jurisdiction. The motion shall be made prior to the attachment of jeopardy. Upon the motion, the juvenile court shall order the probation officer to submit a report on the behavioral patterns and social history of the minor. The report shall include any written or oral statement offered by the victim pursuant to Section 656.2.

(2) In any case in which an individual is alleged to be a person described in Section 602 by reason of the violation, when he or she was 14 or 15-years of age, of any offense listed in subdivision (b), **but was not apprehended prior to the end of juvenile court jurisdiction,** the district attorney or other appropriate prosecuting officer may make a motion to transfer the individual from juvenile court to a court of criminal jurisdiction. The motion shall be made prior to the attachment of jeopardy. Upon the motion, the

juvenile court shall order the probation officer to submit a report on the behavioral patterns and social history of the individual. The report shall include any written or oral statement offered by the victim pursuant to Section 656.2.

(3) Following submission and consideration of the report, and of any other relevant evidence that the petitioner or the minor may wish to submit, the juvenile court shall decide whether the minor should be transferred to a court of criminal jurisdiction. In making its decision, the court shall consider the criteria specified in subparagraphs (A) to (E), inclusive. If the court orders a transfer of jurisdiction, the court shall recite the basis for its decision in an order entered upon the minutes. In any case in which a hearing has been noticed pursuant to this section, the court shall postpone the taking of a plea to the petition until the conclusion of the transfer hearing, and a plea that has been entered already shall not constitute evidence at the hearing.

(A) (i) The degree of criminal sophistication exhibited by the minor.

(ii) When evaluating the criterion specified in clause (i), the juvenile court may give weight to any relevant factor, including, but not limited to, the minor's age, maturity, intellectual capacity, and physical, mental, and emotional health at the time of the alleged offense, the minor's impetuosity or failure to appreciate risks and consequences of criminal behavior, the effect of familial, adult, or peer pressure on the minor's actions, and the effect of the minor's family and community environment and childhood trauma on the minor's criminal sophistication.

(B) (i) Whether the minor can be rehabilitated prior to the expiration of the juvenile court's jurisdiction.

(ii) When evaluating the criterion specified in clause (i), the juvenile court may give weight to any relevant factor, including, but not limited to, the minor's potential to grow and mature.

(C) (i) The minor's previous delinquent history.

(ii) When evaluating the criterion specified in clause (i), the juvenile court may give weight to any relevant factor, including, but not limited to, the seriousness of the minor's previous delinquent history and the effect of the minor's family and community environment and childhood trauma on the minor's previous delinquent behavior.

(D) (i) Success of previous attempts by the juvenile court to rehabilitate the minor.

(ii) When evaluating the criterion specified in clause (i), the juvenile court may give weight to any relevant factor, including, but not limited to, the adequacy of the services previously provided to address the minor's needs.

(E) (i) The circumstances and gravity of the offense alleged in the petition to have been committed by the minor.

(ii) When evaluating the criterion specified in clause (i), the juvenile court may give weight to any relevant factor, including, but not limited to, the actual behavior of the person, the mental state of the person, the person's degree of involvement in the crime, the level of harm actually caused by the person, and the person's mental and emotional development.

(b) This subdivision is applicable to any case in which a minor is alleged to be a person described in Section 602 by reason of the violation of one of the following offenses:

(1) Murder.

(2) Arson, as provided in subdivision (a) or (b) of Section 451 of the Penal Code.

(3) Robbery.

(4) Rape with force, violence, or threat of great bodily harm.

(5) Sodomy by force, violence, duress, menace, or threat of great bodily harm.

(6) A lewd or lascivious act as provided in subdivision (b) of Section 288 of the Penal Code.

(7) Oral copulation by force, violence, duress, menace, or threat of great bodily harm.

(8) An offense specified in subdivision (a) of Section 289 of the Penal Code.

(9) Kidnapping for ransom.

(10) Kidnapping for purposes of robbery.

(11) Kidnapping with bodily harm.

(12) Attempted murder.

(13) Assault with a firearm or destructive device.

(14) Assault by any means of force likely to produce great bodily injury.

(15) Discharge of a firearm into an inhabited or occupied building.

(16) An offense described in Section 1203.09 of the Penal Code.

(17) An offense described in Section 12022.5 or 12022.53 of the Penal Code.

(18) A felony offense in which the minor personally used a weapon described in any provision listed in Section 16590 of the Penal Code.

(19) A felony offense described in Section 136.1 or 137 of the Penal Code.

(20) Manufacturing, compounding, or selling one-half ounce or more of a salt or solution of a controlled substance specified in subdivision (e) of Section 11055 of the Health and Safety Code.

(21) A violent felony, as defined in subdivision (c) of Section 667.5 of the Penal Code, which also would constitute a felony violation of subdivision (b) of Section 186.22 of the Penal Code.

(22) Escape, by the use of force or violence, from a county juvenile hall, home, ranch, camp, or forestry camp in violation of subdivision (b) of Section 871 if great bodily injury is intentionally inflicted upon an employee of the juvenile facility during the commission of the escape.

(23) Torture as described in Sections 206 and 206.1 of the Penal Code.

(24) Aggravated mayhem, as described in Section 205 of the Penal Code.

(25) Carjacking, as described in Section 215 of the Penal Code, while armed with a dangerous or deadly weapon.

(26) Kidnapping for purposes of sexual assault, as punishable in subdivision (b) of Section 209 of the Penal Code.

(27) Kidnapping as punishable in Section 209.5 of the Penal Code.

(28) The offense described in subdivision (c) of Section 26100 of the Penal Code.

(29) The offense described in Section 18745 of the Penal Code.

(30) Voluntary manslaughter, as described in subdivision (a) of Section 192 of the Penal Code.

That portion of §707(a)(2)(b) refers to those situations where the juvenile committed an offense when he or she was 14 or 15-years-old, but was not arrested until after the termination of the juvenile court's jurisdiction, or ages twenty-one, twenty-three, or twenty-five, depending on the nature of the offense (See WIC §607 to 608).

The passage of this bill stirred a great deal of controversy because of certain pending cases, namely in Yolo and Santa Clara counties, is which juveniles age 15 committed brutal homicides. The families of victims and the prosecuting attorneys were incensed by the idea that the youths would be treated as juveniles and would not be justly punished. Several attorneys have threatened to appeal the bill, claiming that it is unconstitutional because it contravenes the will of the people as expressed in their vote on Proposition 57. The outcome remains to be seen at the time of this writing.

The Judicial Waiver

Fitness Hearing Categories

A judicial waiver results from the findings of a special hearing to determine whether the minor is fit to remain within the jurisdiction of the juvenile court. The juvenile court may conduct a **fitness hearing**, at the request of the district attorney, for any minor age 16 or older who is alleged to come within the description of Section 602 WIC, the criminal law violator. This has been the law for many years.

Originally, the minor was presumed to be fit and the burden to "prove" unfitness rested with the prosecutor

These two special fitness categories, found in §707 WIC, **shift the burden of proving fitness to the minor**. One category is for those minors' ages 16 or 17. In this category, if the minor is alleged to have committed any one of the more than 25 serious or violent offenses, as listed, he or she qualifies for a fitness hearing. Originally, the list was called the *dirty dozen* because there were only twelve offenses listed. However, the Legislature has added more offenses each time it has met (see §707 WIC above).

Transfer Hearing (Formerly known as a Fitness Hearing)

Until the passage of SB 1391 on November 8, 2018, minors over the age of 14 charged with a criminal offense would often find themselves directly charged in adult court rather than juvenile court. Prosecutors could, and were often mandated to, directly file charges against juveniles ages 14-17 in adult court. In those cases where the juvenile was 14 years or older, direct file was mandatory under the law for certain serious felonies such as murder and many sex crimes. For other crimes, the prosecution could file the charges against a child as young as 14 directly in adult court under what was known as discretionary direct file. Many of the laws regarding direct file were a result of an earlier proposition passed by California voters in the year 2000, known as Proposition 21. SB 1391 reversed the "get tough on juveniles" sentiment of Proposition 21.

Now under SB 1391, which became the law on November 8, 2018, prosecutors can no longer directly file charges in adult court under any circumstances. The law now requires a hearing before a juvenile court judge before any person who committed a crime while under the age of 18 can be transferred to adult court on criminal charges. Additionally, prior to Proposition 57, the prosecution could move the juvenile court to transfer the matter to adult court in what was called a "fitness hearing" for those juveniles whose case was not "direct filed." The criteria under which juvenile judges were mandated by statute to consider the transfer favored the prosecution. Now, all juveniles ages 16 or 17 charged with a crime will appear before the juvenile court in a **transfer hearing.**

Determining Suitability for Transfer

After hearing all the evidence, the judge must consider five criteria when deciding the minor's fitness (§707 WIC):

A probation officer will have prepared a report for the court addressing these criteria and any relevant information about the minor that might add the judge is determining suitability of the minor to remain in juvenile court.

> ➤ the degree of criminal sophistication exhibited by the minor
> ➤ the minor's previous delinquent history

- the success of any previous attempts by the court to rehabilitate the minor
- the circumstances and gravity of the offense alleged
- whether the minor can be rehabilitated prior to the expiration of the juvenile court's jurisdiction

It should be obvious that the criteria above do not describe characteristics or qualities of the minor in specific or tangible terms. Each one allows for interpretation and judgment. The judge may base his or her decision about the minor's fitness on any one or a combination of these factors.

All the parties will appear in court on the date and time scheduled. Invariably, the minor will be represented by counsel. That attorney will have had discovery; access to the probation officer's report, and to any other relevant information used by the district attorney.

Judicial Finding for Transfer

After considering all the evidence:
- The court may find that the minor is not a fit and proper subject to be dealt with under the juvenile court law if it concludes that the minor would not be amenable to the care, treatment, and training program available through the facilities of the juvenile court... (§707 WIC).

If the minor is found "not a fit and proper subject to be dealt with under juvenile court law...," the minor is an adult from that moment on for purposes of criminal prosecution. He or she may have a jury trial, and receive an adult sentence. The district attorney may file an accusatory pleading (complaint) in adult court charging the minor with a crime, and the case will proceed like any other adult criminal matter. The minor shall be eligible immediately for release on bail or consideration for release on his or her own recognizance.

If the minor turns age 18 while detained in the Hall, he or she may be delivered to the custody of the sheriff for detention in jail unless the court finds that it would be in the best interests of the minor and the public to retain him or her at the Hall.

If the minor is found **to be a fit** and proper subject to remain in juvenile court, the judge will make that finding, and the matter will proceed like any other juvenile case. In this event, the fitness hearing report of the probation officer, which often includes facts about the alleged offense and the minor's feelings about it, will be destroyed; shredded. Once a finding of unfitness is made and the minor is convicted in a criminal court, he or she is presumed to be unfit in any subsequent juvenile proceedings.

Summary

Taken together, over a nine-year period, the U.S. Supreme Court altered forever the nature of juvenile court proceedings. As we have seen in the five appellate cases reviewed in the first portion of this chapter, the court added the constitutional protections of the Fourteenth, Fifth, and most of the Sixth Amendments as a legal overlay to the benevolent protection that a juvenile court allegedly provides.

Juvenile proceedings became more adversarial, and less paternalistic. It is interesting to note how the Court shifted back and forth between interpreting juvenile proceedings as criminal in nature in order to extend many rights to juveniles, and as civil proceedings in order not to extend them other rights, such as the right to a jury trial.

The second portion of this chapter described the methods by which the jurisdiction of a juvenile case can be waived, and the matter handled in criminal court as an adult case. Three types of waivers were discussed: **judicial waiver**, in which the judge decides fitness, after holding a fitness hearing; **legislative waiver**, by which the legislature has mandated that certain types of offenses shall be tried in criminal court; **Of significance is the recent change in juvenile court** law prohibiting any minor under the age of sixteen years from entering the adult criminal system. This represents a shift back to rehabilitation, at least for the younger minors.

These procedures detailed in the several subsections of §707 WIC reflected a *get-tough* approach by the legislature in responding to serious and violent offenses committed by juveniles. This is particularly so in the waiver methods provided for by Proposition 21. An increasing number of juveniles will undoubtedly find themselves in criminal court facing adult trials and harsh penalties. Whether this results in reducing delinquency or creating a younger breed of criminal, remains to be seen.

References

Bellinger, Martha E., "Waiving Goodbye to Waiver for Serious Juvenile Offenders: A Proposal to Revamp California's Fitness Statute," Journal *of Juvenile Law*, Vol. 11, No. 1 (1990), pp. 1-16.

Cavin, Jeffrey D., "Waiver of a Juvenile's Fifth and Sixth Amendment Rights," *Journal of Juvenile Law*, Vol. 13 (1992), pp. 27-41.

Datig, Craig. *Proposition 21: The Impact on Juvenile Court Operations*. An unpublished monograph presented in Sacramento, CA. at the April 7, 2000 Annual Conference of the California Association of Administration of Justice Educators.

Platt, Anthony. *The Child Savers*. Chicago: University of Chicago Press, 1969

Case Decisions

Breed v. Jones (1975) 421 U. S. 519

Guillory v. Superior Court (2003) Cal 4th

In re Gault (1967) 387 U. S. 1

In re Roger S. (1977) 19 CA 3d 921

In re Scott K. (1979) 24 CA 3d 395

In re Steven C. (1970) 9 CA 3d 255; 88 Cal. Rptr. 97

In re Winship (1970) 397 U. S. 358

Kent v. U. S. (1966) 383 U. S. 541

McKeiver v. Pennsylvania (1971) 403 U. S. 528

Chapter 7: Pre-Court Procedures

Key Terms and Concepts

Affidavit
Allegations
Civil proceeding
Detention
Detention criteria
Detention hearing
Discretion
Discretionary release
District attorney

Home supervision
Intake Officer
Informal probation
Juvenile court
Juvenile hall
Non-detention petition
Petition
Prima facie case
Promise to appear (PTA)

Introduction

The juvenile court is a division of the Superior Court of a county, with a Superior Court Judge appointed annually by the Court's presiding judge to serve on the juvenile bench. The size of the court depends directly on the size of the population served. In large urban cities, there may be several judges sitting full time, whereas in a lightly populated rural county, one judge might sit only one full day or less per week.

In most counties, the judges are assisted by a court referee or commissioner. These are attorneys, appointed by the judge to serve full time in his or her capacity, but with limited jurisdiction. These referees or commissioners hear most of the preliminary matters and uncontested cases, while the judge devotes his or her efforts to hearing the more serious or contested cases. Also, any order removing a minor from the physical custody of a parent must be signed by the judge. In the material that follows, the word *court* is often used interchangeably with the word *judge*.

All juvenile court hearings are civil proceedings, just as they have always been, even though now many of the constitutional protections afforded criminal suspects apply. Proceedings are initiated by a **petition** filed on behalf of a minor by the district attorney alleging that the minor comes within the description of Section 602 WIC "in that said minor did violate the law" (the specific law is stated). The petition also is a request that the court declare the minor to be a ward of the court; to sit in *loco parentis* as the substitute parent.

The probation officer of the county (in most counties) is appointed by the juvenile court judge and, along with the assistant and deputy probation officers, serves as the investigative and enforcement arms of the court. Consequently, any minor cited or delivered by police to the probation officer under §626 WIC is actually delivered to the court. And, by making this referral, police are requesting that a petition be filed in court. The police may not file the petition, only the DA has this authority.

In many instances the minors referred to probation by police are often handled informally rather than by direct court action. Therefore, this chapter focuses on those procedures leading up to, and/or used as alternatives to court.

It is estimated that 40 percent to 50 percent of the juveniles taken into temporary custody by law enforcement officers are handled informally by the officers, and never reach court. Of those referred to court by police, approximately 40 percent are handled by probation in some manner short of formal court proceedings. Consequently, the juveniles who find themselves before the court usually are repeat offenders, serious offenders, probation violators, or those who deny their offenses.

Probation: Organization and Functions

Probation work is organized around the concept of functional specialization, similar to that of police, with the larger organizations having the work divided up into many functional units. Officers within these units work for the court and serve as either the investigative or the enforcement arm of the court.

The typical probation department will have at least an Intake Unit, a Court Investigation Unit, a Field Supervision Unit, and a Placement Unit. The larger the organization, the more numerous the work units. The role of the Intake officer is the primary focus of this chapter.

The Role of Probation Intake

Officers working in the Intake Unit receive the case from police and initiate any proceedings to follow. They are sometimes nicknamed "gatekeepers" because they often decide who gets into the court system.

In some counties, Intake staff is on duty around the clock to receive and screen juvenile referrals immediately after delivery by law enforcement. Those counties not having an Intake officer on duty after 5:00 p.m. might have a deputized night shift supervisor at the Hall with the authority to receive the case and make the initial decision as to release or detention. However, if no Intake officer is on duty when a minor is delivered, he or she might be *dressed in* (showered and dressed in Hall clothes), and sent to a living unit until an Intake officer is available.

Intake is responsible for making several important decisions. First, Intake must **advise a minor** of his or her Fifth and Sixth Amendment rights. Secondly, Intake must decide if further detention of the minor really is necessary. Juveniles do not have the constitutional right to bail (***Baldwin v. Lewis, 1969***), and California is one of about 40 states that make no provision for juveniles to bail or to be released on their own recognizance. Consequently, **discretionary release** to a parent or guardian by Intake is the only alternative to the continued detention in a juvenile hall for the minor pending court.

Upon delivery to the probation officer of a minor who has been taken into temporary custody:

> ...the probation officer shall **immediately investigate** the circumstances of the minor and the facts surrounding his being taken into custody and shall **immediately release** such minor to the custody of his parent, guardian, or responsible relative unless one or more of the following (8) conditions exist:
>
> ✓ the minor is in need of proper and effective parental care or control and has no parent, guardian, or responsible relative willing (or able) to exercise... such care or control...
>
> ✓ the minor is destitute or is not provided with the necessities of life or is not provided with a home or suitable place of abode
>
> ✓ the minor is provided with a home which is an unfit place for him by reason of neglect, cruelty, or depravity or physical abuse

- ✓ continued detention of the minor is a matter of immediate and urgent necessity for the protection of the minor or reasonable necessity for the protection of the person or property of another

- ✓ the minor is likely to flee the jurisdiction of the court

- ✓ the minor has violated an order of the juvenile court

- ✓ the minor is physically dangerous to the public because of a mental or physical deficiency, disorder, or abnormality.

- ✓ the minor used a firearm in the commission of the alleged offense

Even though the W & I Code requires the probation officer to immediately advise the minor of his or her rights, the initial investigation by Intake must focus on the need to detain the minor in the Hall pending further proceedings. Consequently, some Intake officers do not complete the advisement requirements until after deciding detention status and then, only if they are going to question the minor about the alleged offense. This seems to be flouting the law rather than fulfilling it.

Intake must release the minor to a parent, guardian, or responsible relative unless one of the criteria above is met. If the minor is released, but Intake wants the minor and the parents to return for a further discussion of the case, Intake may require the minor and/or the responsible adult to sign a written **promise to appear** (PTA) at a designated date and time.

Proposition 21 amended §629 WIC to require that a minor age 14 years or older, who is alleged to have committed or attempted to commit a felony, **shall not be released until** the minor and a parent, guardian, or relative both have signed a written promise to appear.

Intake may release a minor to his or her parents, guardian, or responsible adult even if the minor does meet one of the criteria set forth above in §628 WIC. In this case, however, the minor shall be required to sign an agreement to participate in a form of release called **Home Supervision**. The minor will be released, but with conditions on his or her conduct, and with supervision by a probation officer.

The responsibilities of the supervising probation officer are to enforce these conditions and to return the minor to detention if he or she violates any of them. These conditions may include curfew and school attendance, and any other requirements necessary for the protection of the minor or the person or property of others, or to insure the minor's appearances in court.

Once the decision has been made about the minor's detention or release, Intake will investigate the case to determine what further action, if any, is appropriate. At this point, the authority of Intake is controlled by specific legal criteria.

If the police or any other referring agency or person allege that the offense committed by the minor would be a misdemeanor if committed by an adult, Intake has full discretion on how to proceed. However, **Intake must prepare an affidavit to be taken to the district attorney within 48 hours** (refer the case to the district attorney for the decision), if the minor:

➢ has been referred to the probation officer for any violation of an offense listed in Section 707 WIC (b), (d)(2) or (e)

➢ is under 14 years of age at the date of the offense and that the offense constitutes a second felony referral to the probation officer

➢ was 14 years of age or older at the date of the offense and that the offense constitutes a felony referral to the probation officer

➢ has been referred to the probation officer for the sale or possession for sale of a controlled drug or narcotic

➢ has been referred to the probation officer for possession or sale of marijuana that takes place at a public or private school

➢ has been referred to the probation officer for a gang crime (§186.22 PC)

➢ has previously been placed in a program of informal probation

➢ if the minor has committed an offense in which the restitution owed to the victim exceeds one thousand dollars ($1,000)

Intake will refer any case that meets the above descriptions to the district attorney with a recommendation on how to proceed, but it is the DA who makes the final decision.

The Discretion of Intake

If none of these eight criteria apply, Intake has full authority to:
- dismiss the case

- place the minor on informal supervision

- refer the case to the district attorney with a request for a petition to bring the matter to court

Before reaching one of these decisions Intake will discuss the case with the juvenile and the parents. If it is a petty offense or if it is situational and not likely to recur or there are parental strengths in the home, and no restitution is owing, Intake might dismiss it.

If it is the type of case that does not need full court action, but some sort of supervision seems necessary, Intake may have the minor voluntarily consent to a period of 6 months **informal probation**. The minor must sign a written consent, and in doing so, the minor waives time for a speedy adjudication hearing (trial).

During this 6-month period the minor and/or his or her parents may be required to participate in some form of counseling or education, and to comply with other relevant conditions. The minor might also be required to participate in a shelter care or residential treatment program for up to 90 days. A probation officer will be assigned to the case to ensure the compliance of the minor and his or her parents to the requirements, and to help the minor with any problems or conditions that might contribute to his or her continuing delinquent activity.

Intake will usually request a petition if prior efforts to direct the minor have not been effective, or if Intake thinks that formal court action is warranted. If Intake requests a petition from the district attorney, he or she is required to complete an affidavit supporting the request, which will be attached to the petition.

If Intake does not refer the matter to the district attorney for a petition, he or she must inform the referring police (or other) agency of that decision within 21 days. Thereafter, the referring agency has 30 days to appeal the probation officer's decision to the district attorney.

In any case in which the Intake officer refers the matter to the District Attorney, either for a petition or because the case fits one of the eight criteria listed above, Intake will recommend what action is appropriate.

The Discretion of the District Attorney

The county district attorney is defined under the Government Code as the public prosecutor. Even though juvenile proceedings are not criminal in nature the district attorney has the complete and exclusive discretion to decide whether a **petition** should be filed with the court. The petition is a legal document that contains the **allegations** (charges). It is also a legal request for the court to declare the minor a ward of the court.

When AB 3121 took effect in 1976, removing status offenders from the formal system, it also moved the juvenile court a step or two away from the concept of *parens patriae* by adding the §707 offenses and by introducing the district attorney into the proceedings with 602s. This gave the civil nature of a benevolent court an overlay of the adversary proceedings found in criminal court. Before 1976, a probation officer was assigned to present the case in court; to prosecute, as it were.

A deputy district attorney assigned to juvenile court will review the case and the recommendation of the Intake officer, and may then exercise one of several options similar to those of Intake:

➢ dismiss

➢ refer the case back to Intake to proceed with informal supervision

➢ file a petition

Steps Toward Adjudication

The Petition

The petition to declare a minor a ward of the court under §602 WIC is filed by the deputy district attorney assigned to juvenile court. Those familiar with criminal procedures would know that in adult criminal court the DA files a **complaint against** a defendant containing criminal charges. In juvenile procedures the wording is different.

The DA files a **petition on behalf of** a minor which contains **allegations** that bring the minor within the description of §602 WIC.

The petition may be of two types: a **non-detention** or a **detention** petition. If the DA files a non-detention petition, it will mean that the minor must go to court to face the allegations, but will remain home to await the court date, usually in about 30 days. A detention petition means that the minor will go to court, and that the DA wants the minor to remain in the Hall, pending court.

To comply with the Gault decision, the minor and his or her parents or attorney must be served a copy of the petition and Notice of Hearing in person, or by certified mail, within 5 days of the hearing, if the minor is detained, and within 10 days if not detained.

The petition must include the following:

- name of the court and title of the proceeding
- code section/s and subdivision/s under which proceedings are initiated
- the name, age, and address of the minor
- names and addresses of both parents, guardian or responsible adult
- a concise statement of the facts of the offense
- whether the minor is detained, and if detained, the exact date and time the minor was taken into custody
- a notice to whomever is responsible for the support of the minor
- whether the offense alleged would be a felony or misdemeanor if committed by an adult
- a statement advising that the minor and parents or guardian are entitled to have an attorney present at all court hearings, and that one will be appointed to those unable to afford one

In addition to the petition, the court may issue a citation directing any parent, guardian, or foster parent to appear at the time and place indicated. If these individuals do not respond to the citation and appear, or if the court thinks that the citation will be ineffective, it may issue an arrest warrant. The court may also issue an arrest warrant for any minor not detained if the behavior of the minor will endanger self or others. If the DA files a detention petition, the matter must be scheduled in court for a detention hearing.

The Detention Hearing

The court referee or commissioner usually hears detention hearings each morning. If the DA files a detention petition alleging what amounts to a felony, the minor must appear in court for a **detention hearing** the next judicial day after the petition is filed; or within 48 hours after the filing of a petition if the allegation is a misdemeanor, excluding non-judicial days.

This 48-hour time period was challenged in ***Alfredo A. v. Superior Court, 1993***. The minor was taken into custody without a warrant in July 1991, pursuant to sections 602 and 625 WIC, on suspicion of possessing cocaine base for sale. He claimed that the constitutional rules that apply to adults in detention apply to juveniles as well.

The U.S. Supreme Court had previously held that in adult cases of a warrantless arrest, the adult is entitled to a probable cause hearing on the legality of his or her arrest within 48 hours of arrest, with no exception for non-judicial days. (***People v. McLaughlin, 1991***). Alfredo claimed that this same right applied in juvenile cases.

In May 1993 the California Supreme Court held by a 4 to 3 vote that the *McLaughlin rule* did not apply to juvenile proceedings. In the Court's view there was more involved in the detention of juveniles than the issue of Fourth Amendment protection. The state has an interest in helping and guiding juveniles as well as guaranteeing their rights. The court ruled that juveniles do have the right of judicial determination of the legality of their arrest without a warrant, but this may be held within 72 hours of arrest with no exception for non-judicial days.

The purpose of a detention hearing is to have the judge, referee, or commissioner **determine if further detention is necessary**, as a check on the DA's decision. When the minor and his or her parents appear in court, the referee must advise them of the nature of the allegation/s and of their rights to be represented by an attorney at every stage of the proceedings. If the minor and/or his or her parents want an attorney but cannot afford one, one will be appointed by the court. If the minor wants an attorney, but the parents who can afford one will not hire one for the minor, the court will appoint one at the expense of the parents.

The issue of a minor's right to effective counsel is so important that the court might appoint an attorney to represent the minor even if the parents retain private counsel. This will occur when the court observes a conflict of interest between the *real* best interests of the minor and the parents' interests in what happens to the minor. The thinking here is that an attorney represents whomever pays the bill. Consequently, an attorney hired by the parents, works for the interests of the minor as translated by the parents, whereas a court appointed attorney works independently for the minor. A minor and/or the parents may waive their rights to counsel if the court finds that they knowingly and intelligently made the waiver.

Criteria for Detention

The juvenile court judge, referee, or commissioner is guided in his or her decision to order continued detention for the minor by the same criteria previously mentioned when discussing the discretion of Intake. If it appears that the minor has not violated a court order, is not an escapee from a court commitment, is not likely to flee the jurisdiction of the court, or that it is not of immediate and urgent necessity for the protection of the minor, or reasonably necessary for the protection of the person or property of another, the court shall release the minor.

The phrases ***immediate and urgent necessity*** and ***reasonably necessary*** are vague concepts open to interpretation. The referee may consider the circumstance and gravity of the alleged offense in reaching a decision. Consequently, the judge conducting this hearing has considerable discretion in reaching his or her decision. The court must state on the record its reason for ordering detention, but preventive detention is legal (***Schall v. Martin*, 1984**).

If the court finds that one or more of the detention criteria apply, it may release the minor to a parent or guardian under **Home Supervision**, with conditions, for a period of 15 days. This time may be extended or modified from time to time until the case is settled. The court may also order the minor released from the Hall to be housed in a non-secure facility either run by or under contract with the probation department.

If the court does not want the minor released it may order the minor detained in the Hall for a period not to exceed 15 days. The case will be set for the adjudication hearing (trial) within that 15-day period. Continuances may be granted by the court, but only for good cause, and usually for no longer than a week at a time. The court is very reluctant to delay juvenile hearings, especially if the minor is detained.

Effective January 2004, §207.6 WIC was modified allowing the juvenile court judge or referee to order the detention of a minor in an adult jail or facility only if all of the following apply:

- ➢ the petition contains allegations that the minor committed what would be a serious or violent felony if committed by an adult

- ➢ the court makes its findings on the record

- ➢ the court finds that the minor poses a danger to the staff, other minors in a juvenile facility or the public because of his or her failure to respond to disciplinary control of the juvenile facility or because the nature of the danger posed cannot be safely managed by the disciplinary procedures of a juvenile facility

Detention: The Juvenile Hall

The juvenile hall is a self-contained facility in which a minor may eat, sleep, attend school, recreate, and worship. Almost all the 50 counties in California have a Hall to detain minors pending court, or pending placement after court. The populations in these Halls ranges from 10 to 15 in one of the rural counties, to a county like Los Angeles which has three Halls, each holding approximately 600 to 900 minors at any one time.

Some of the county Halls have what is called a commitment program, where selected minors are sent from court to complete some sort of rehabilitation program. Otherwise, a Hall is a place of detention, similar to a jail for adults. The job of the youth supervisors is to maintain custody and control, not to provide rehabilitative services. In the words of one supervisor, their job is "to keep them there, and keep them tired." A tired youth has less energy to cause problems.

The larger the facility, the stronger the custody orientation, and the more regimented the programs. Nevertheless, if the reader has any idea of working with juveniles in any capacity, working in a Hall as a youth supervisor will provide an invaluable experience and insight into the system.

Establishing a Prima Facie Case

If the minor or his or her attorney requests that the DA establish what is termed a ***prima facie* case**, the matter must be scheduled for a hearing within three to five days following the detention hearing. This proceeding would be similar to, but not exactly like, a preliminary hearing in an adult felony case. To establish a *prima facie* case, the DA must present sufficient evidence which, when uncontested, will prove the facts alleged.

One purpose by the defense attorney in requesting a *prima facie* case is to later challenge the admissibility of the evidence. This occurs when the defense believes that the evidence was seized illegally, by an illegal warrant, arrest, or search. If the defense is successful in getting that evidence suppressed, the DA might not be able to establish the elements necessary for a *prima facie* case. In that event, the petition is dismissed and the case is over.

If the results of a *prima facie* or suppression hearing are favorable for the district attorney, the case will be set for the juvenile court hearings to follow. Pending the outcome of these hearings, the minor might be detained in juvenile hall, released to his or her parents without conditions, or released on Home Supervision, which will include conditions his or her behavior, and supervision by a probation officer.

Summary

This chapter examined the juvenile court, as a division of the superior court of a county, and the fact that juvenile court hearings are still civil proceedings. The preliminary procedures leading up to the actual court hearings were described, including the role of the Intake probation officer, as *gatekeeper* to the system, and that of the district attorney, the individual with the sole authority to file a petition. The chapter ended with a description of a hearing in which the district attorney might have to establish a *prima facie* case to prove that there is sufficient evidence to proceed with the rest of the court process. The chapter to follow details that process and the various consequences the juvenile might face.

Internet References

http://www.leginfo.ca.gov/calaw.html

http://www.leginfo.ca.gov/cgibin/calawquery?codesection=wic&codebod y=&hits=20

http://findlaw.com/cacases/

Case Decisions

Alfredo A. v. Superior Court (1993) 5 Cal. 4th; and Cal. Supreme Court, No S024618, January 24, 1994.

Baldwin v. Lewis (1969) USDC (E.D. Wisconsin)

People v. McLaughlin (1991) 111 S. CT. 1661

Schall v. Martin (1984) 467 U.S. 253

Chapter 8: Juvenile Court Proceedings

Key Terms and Concepts

Admission of the public
Adjudicate
Adjudication Hearing
Allegation
Bifurcated hearing process
Camp commitment
Citation Hearing
Court commitment

Clear and convincing evidence
Defense strategies
Deferred judgment
Disposition
Dispositional hearing
DJF Commitment
Family reunification
Finding of fact
Informal probation

Judicial finding
Jurisdictional hearing
Out-of-home placement
Probation conditions
Probation investigation
Probation officer's report
Rehabilitation model
Reunification
Supplemental petition

Introduction

Proceedings in juvenile court are **bifurcated**. That is, they are divided into two stages, the adjudication hearing and the dispositional hearing, which are similar to the adult stages of trial and sentencing. The **adjudication hearing** is a fact-finding hearing similar to an adult trial, for the purpose of determining if the allegations of the petition are true or not. It is also called a **jurisdictional hearing** in some counties because the court determines whether it has jurisdiction in the case, along with adjudicating the case. The **dispositional stage** is similar to the sentencing hearing in adult cases.

There is a newly created procedure called **deferred entry of judgment**. When that procedure is used, the adjudication/jurisdictional and dispositional hearings are postponed pending the minor's successful completion of probation supervision.

This chapter examines these bifurcated hearings as to their nature, purpose, and outcome, including the typical dispositions a court usually will make.

The Adjudication/Jurisdictional Hearing

The **adjudication/jurisdictional hearing** usually is held within fifteen days of the detention hearing, if the minor is detained, and thirty days if the minor has been home, pending the hearing. It will be useful to cite §680 WIC because it describes the intended nature and purpose of the adjudication hearing:

> ➤ The judge of the juvenile court shall control all proceedings during the hearing with a view to the expeditious and effective ascertainment of the jurisdictional facts and the ascertainment of all information relative to the present condition and future welfare of the person upon whose behalf the petition is brought. Except where there is a contested issue of fact, or law, the proceedings shall be conducted in an informal non-adversary atmosphere with a view to obtaining the maximum cooperation of the minor upon whose behalf the petition is brought ...

The Hearing Process

The hearing begins with an explanation of the **allegations**, the nature of the hearing, and the possible consequences. The judge shall inquire if all parties understand their rights to an attorney, and the court will appoint counsel when appropriate.

If the matter is uncontested and the minor admits that the allegations are true, the judge will make a **finding of fact** that the minor is a person described in §602 WIC, and will **sustain** the petition. Frequently, the defense and the prosecutor will have worked out a plea bargain, and the petition will be adjusted to reflect the new allegations that the minor will admit.

If the matter is contested and the defense has not yet challenged the admissibility of the evidence, the defense may make a motion for a **suppression hearing**. This will be heard before the adjudication begins (before jeopardy attaches). The outcome of a suppression hearing might determine whether the prosecution has a case left to proceed to adjudication.

A contested case proceeds like a trial in that the attorneys give opening statements, present their sides of the case then give closing arguments. California is one of about 40 states that **does not provide for a jury trial** in juvenile court. The hearing is conducted by a judge sitting alone.

At the conclusion of the case presented by the DA, the court may on its own motion or one by the defense, find that the evidence is not sufficient to sustain the petition or the court may lessen the degree of the offense alleged. If this motion is not made or if it is made but not sustained, the defense will present evidence on behalf of the minor's defense. If a minor is under the age of 14 years the court must also find that the minor has the capacity to understand the nature and consequences of his or her act. This finding must be by a standard of proof known as **clear and convincing evidence** (*In re* **Manuel L., 1993**).

Defense Strategies

A defense attorney in a contested matter will approach the prosecution's case with one of the following three strategy categories.

➤ The offense alleged did not occur, or at least it did not occur at the degree alleged.

The strategy here is either to create such a reasonable doubt that the judge must find the allegations not true or to lower the degree of the offense to some lessor, but included allegation. One or more specific defenses will be put forward by defense counsel in using this strategy:

- ✓ the minor did not have guilty knowledge of an offense
- ✓ the minor lacked the specific intent
- ✓ the victim consented
- ✓ the minor is of such good character that he or she could not possibly have committed such an act

➤ If the alleged act did occur, the minor did not commit it. Someone else did.

This would be a case where the evidence might prove that the act occurred but is weak in connecting the act with the minor. The defense will claim such things as:

- ✓ an alibi
- ✓ the minor was framed by the real offender
- ✓ mistaken identification, the identification process was tainted by the police procedures

> The alleged act did occur but it was not an offense because the minor has a legal excuse. From this position the defense will attempt to prove such things as:
> - ✓ self-defense
> - ✓ accident or misfortune
> - ✓ the minor was acting under threat or duress
> - ✓ entrapment
> - ✓ the minor was insane when he or she did the act
> - ✓ the minor is under the age of 14 and lacks the capacity to commit a criminal act pursuant to Penal Code Section 26

In a statutory rape case involving a 17-year-old male and a 12-year-old female, the U.S. Supreme Court ruled that "mistake of age" is not a valid defense that can be presented in court (***U.S. v. Juvenile Male, 2000***). It is not necessary for the prosecution to prove whether the offender knew the age of the victim.

If the minor does not contest doing the act but merely claims insanity while committing the act, the court will conduct only one hearing on the question of sanity. In either case when the defense claims insanity the judge alone hears the evidence and makes a finding. If the judge finds that the minor was not insane, the case continues, as would any other delinquency proceeding. If the court finds that the minor was insane at the time of the alleged offense the minor will be committed to a hospital or to an out-patient treatment clinic until his or her sanity is restored. In the case of a felony allegation the minor must spend at least 180 days in a hospital before being released to out-patient status. When the court is convinced that the minor's sanity is restored the petition will be dismissed and the minor released.

The Finding

After the presentation of all the evidence the judge makes a decision as to whether the allegations in the petition were **proven beyond a reasonable doubt**. This is called a **finding of fact** and is the equivalent to a verdict in an adult trial. The allegations are either **true or not true**. In a sense, this wording moves the juvenile back one step from being held fully responsible. Note the words used in the finding: the juvenile is not found guilty, the wording (allegation) in the petition is true. If the finding is that the allegation is not true, the petition is dismissed and the minor is released. If the judge finds that the **allegation is true**, he or she will sustain the petition and set the matter on calendar for the second phase of the proceedings, the dispositional hearing.

In those cases where the alleged offense could be either a felony or a misdemeanor (wobbler) if committed by an adult, the court must declare which level the offense will be.

Admission of the Public

In the appellate case decisions reviewed in Chapter 6, the U.S. Supreme Court extended many constitutional rights to juveniles but it did not give them the right to a public or jury trial. The states were left to establish their own procedures. Ten states provide for a jury trial and several others have some provision for public admission to a juvenile hearing.

In California a minor and his or her parent/s or guardian may request that the public be allowed to attend. Without their request, "…the public shall not be admitted to a juvenile court hearing." However, as authorized by Penal Code Section 868.5, any prosecution witness may have the attendance of two family members for support.

After having said that, §676 WIC states that a judge or referee may "…admit those persons he or she deem to have a direct and legitimate interest in the particular case or the work of the court." In addition, the public will be admitted on the same basis as they may be admitted to criminal trials if it is alleged that the minor committed a serious or violent felony (§707 WIC) or a street gang offense.

It was mentioned earlier in this chapter that juvenile court proceedings are bifurcated. That is, they are divided into two phases. Upon completion of the adjudication/ jurisdictional hearing, the petition is either dismissed and everyone goes home, or the petition is sustained and the matter is scheduled for a dispositional hearing. We will examine that court process in the remaining portion of this chapter.

The Dispositional Process

A dispositional hearing in juvenile court is procedurally very similar to a sentencing hearing in adult court, although there is dramatic difference in the stated purposes of each. Before the dispositional process itself is examined, it will be useful to understand just what the California Legislature intended as the purpose of juvenile court law.

Purposes of Juvenile Court Law

The purpose of juvenile court law and the legislative limits placed on possible dispositions that a judge may make are found in §202 WIC:

- to provide for the **protection and safety** of the public and each minor

- to preserve and strengthen the minor's *family ties* whenever possible, removing the minor from the custody of his or her parents only when necessary for his or her welfare or for the safety and protection of the public

- **reunification** of the minor with his or her family shall be a primary objective if the minor is removed from the home

- to secure for the minor **custody, care, and discipline** as nearly as possible equivalent to that which should have been given by his or her parents

- to hold minors **accountable** for their behavior, and assure that appropriate **punishment** for their circumstances is consistent with the **rehabilitative objectives** the court

- to reaffirm that the **duty of a parent** to support and maintain a minor child continues, subject to the financial ability of the parent to pay during any period in which the minor may be removed from the custody of the parent

In using the term *punishment,* the law means the imposition of sanctions which include the following:
- payment of a fine by the minor
- rendering of community service without compensation
- limitations on the minor's liberty imposed as a condition of probation
- commitment of the minor to a local detention or treatment facility

Punishment Does Not Include Retribution

The purposes of the juvenile court are quite clear: protection and safety of the public and the safety and rehabilitation of the minor. All **dispositions must serve those purposes to be legal**. They also must not be in conflict with the Constitutions of the State or United States.

Two models currently are in conflict at this dispositional stage: The **Rehabilitation Model** and the **Justice Model**. Before 1976 the Rehabilitation Model was the exclusive approach taken with juveniles. They were not responsible for their acts and needed the court's protection and treatment. The passage of AB 3121, effective in 1976, added two additional purposes:

- to protect the public from criminal conduct by minors
- to impose on the minor a sense of responsibility for his own acts

This corresponded to an increasing "get tough" public approach with adult offenders that began about the same time. Along with this, university academics originated the concept known as the Justice Model to characterize a paradigm that emphasizes individual responsibility, fairness, and punishment for a crime rather than treatment.

There is no conflict between the two philosophies in wanting to be fair or imposing a sense of responsibility on a minor for his or her acts. However, conflict arises when one pursues a plan of individualized treatment for each minor while at the same time punishes like minors for like offenses. In theory the legislature and the system stressed protection for the public and treatment for the minor and did not include punishment as a purpose until 1984.

The dispositional hearing must be set either within 15 days after the adjudication hearing, if the minor is detained or within 30 days if not detained. During this period between the two hearings the case is **referred to the probation** officer to conduct a social study and prepare a **report** for the court. This includes a detailed explanation of the offense, the minor's social and personal background, and a recommendation to the judge as to the appropriate treatment plan.

The Probation Officer's Report

The case is assigned by a probation supervisor to a deputy probation officer who works in the **Investigation Unit**. Assignments are distributed among the officers in order to equalize their workloads. Assignments are either based on some standard of time required to complete a specific type of investigation or on the total number of cases each officer has completed so far during the month. Each officer will investigate approximately 18 to 24 cases per month.

During the investigation, the probation officer will read the police report, and any court transcripts, along with the files of the district attorney, and will interview the minor, the victim, witnesses, the parent/s, school officials, and any other persons having relevant information. If the minor is on probation or parole, the probation officer will read the probation file and will discuss the minor's adjustment on probation or parole with the appropriate officer or agent. Institutional records also might be read.

The probation officer's report concludes with a recommendation to the judge as to a disposition that would be in the best interests of the minor and the community. Sometimes, however, it represents what would have the least detrimental effect on the minor.

The Dispositional Hearing

This hearing is usually more informal than the adjudication hearing. The judge controls the proceedings but he or she must consider all relevant evidence (*In re J.L.P.*, **1972**). The judge begins the hearing by stating that he or she has read and considered the report of the probation officer, and any other written documents presented by either the district attorney or the defense attorney.

The hearing might become adversary in nature if the prosecution or defense disagrees with the probation officer's report and recommendation. The probation officer sits as an arm of the court, as the **court's investigator**. The judge relies heavily on his or her recommendation and will order what the probation officer recommends in most cases. However, the defense attorney often will argue for a less restrictive disposition, while the DA will argue for a more restrictive one.

The victim is invited to appear at the dispositional hearing if the offense was an act which would be a felony if committed by an adult, and the victim may, at the court's discretion, express his or her views about the offense and disposition.

The judge will consider a number of **factors,** such as:

- the gravity of the offense
- the circumstances and nature of the offense
- the age, attitude, and sophistication of the minor
- the prior record and responses to prior grants of probation
- the strengths and weaknesses in the parental home
- the minor's progress and behavior in school
- any loss or harm to the victim
- community resources
- the needs of the community for safety and protection

After considering all the relevant information the judge will make a **disposition** (sentence) in the case which the law requires to be the **least restrictive alternative**, providing that it is in the best interests of the minor and the community. However, as of March 8, 2000, §707(d)(5) WIC states that if the district attorney could have directly filed the case in criminal court, but elected to file in juvenile court, and the 602 petition is sustained, the minor **must be committed** to some type of secure facility for some period of time. No minimum time is required.

The following represents the dispositions allowed by law and are the ones most frequently ordered by the court:

- **Informal Probation**: If the minor meets the criteria set out in §654 WIC, the court may place the minor on a period of 6 months informal probation without declaring him or her a ward. Conditions of that probation may include:

  - an order that the minor attend school
  - a curfew requiring the minor to be at his or her residence between certain given hours, unless accompanied by a parent
  - an order requiring the parents or guardian to participate with the minor in an appropriate program of counseling or education

Other conditions related to the treatment needs of the minor may be ordered and might include restricting peer associations, especially gang members, a prohibition against wearing gang colors, restitution to a victim, electronic monitoring, and the 3-way search clause.

If the minor violates a condition of this probation the judge may declare the minor to be a ward of the court and may proceed with another disposition. If the minor completes informal probation and no further supervision is needed, supervision will terminate and the case (allegation) will be dismissed.

> **Wardship:** The court may declare the minor to be a ward of the court, which gives the court almost complete control over the minor. The court then sits in *loco parentis*. It has become the substitute parent. The court's authority is given as follows:

> ✓ may make **any** and all reasonable orders for the care, supervision, custody, conduct, maintenance, and support of the minor

> ✓ medical treatment may be ordered over the wishes of the parents, even if their wishes are based on religious beliefs

At the discretion of the court the minor may be placed on probation with appropriate conditions, but without supervision, unless the minor has committed burglary (§459 P.C.), possession of any controlled drug or narcotic (11350 H & S), or any one of the fitness hearing offenses listed in §707 WIC.

In approximately 85 percent of the cases, the minor will be adjudged a ward of the court, placed on formal supervised probation, and placed in the physical custody of a parent or guardian. The court may order the parents to participate in any appropriate counseling or education program, and may limit the control that a parent or guardian may exercise over the minor.

There was a time when the court would order probation conditions such as: *avoid all evil associations.* Wording of this type has been found to be unconstitutional, based on the ***void-for-vagueness*** doctrine.

The court is reluctant to remove a minor from the physical custody of his or her natural parent/s unless that placement is really detrimental to the minor. Legally, the court may not make such an order unless the court finds that either:

➤ the parents are incapable of providing or have failed to provide for the minor
➤ the minor has been tried on probation and has failed to reform
➤ the welfare of the; minor requires that he or she be taken from the custody of the parent or guardian

Out-of-Home Placement

If the minor is placed in a **foster home**, the home must be licensed or certified. Usually the same probation conditions will apply and probation supervision will continue. However, supervision might be by an officer working in the **Placement Unit** rather than the regular Supervision Unit. The county must pay for the cost of the minor's placement, although the parents will be ordered to reimburse the county for some portion of that cost based on their ability to pay.

A minor might be placed in a **24-hour residential facility** rather than in a foster home. It depends on the needs of the minor and the resources available. This could include some local treatment facility, or an out-of-town or out-of-state residential program. A number of counties place wards in residential programs in Nevada, Arizona, New Mexico, and Utah. The cost for each placement runs $4,000 to $8,000 per month. This type of care, after the fact, is far more expensive than what early prevention efforts might have cost.

Placing a minor in one of these programs could create substantial liability for a county if a program does not maintain health and safety standards to protect a minor. Any such placement should receive continuous monitoring by the county agency.

County Camp, Ranch, or School Commitments

Many counties have one or more local ranches, camps, or school programs where minors can be committed for short periods of rehabilitation. These programs vary in size from a single 20-bed probation camp in Sonoma County to approximately twenty 100-bed camps in Los Angeles County. They are usually run by the county probation department, and the minor is on probation during his or her stay at the facility.

A commitment to a ranch, school, or camp is not a final disposition, like an adult sentence would be. Rather, it is ordered as a condition of probation. However, a minor may **not be confined** for any offense longer than an adult could be for the same crime. The juvenile wards are assigned to the caseload of a supervising probation officer, often called the camp/ranch/school officer. The minor will continue under probation supervision in the community upon his or her release from camp until the court decides to terminate its jurisdiction, or until age 21, whichever comes first. As a practical matter, court jurisdiction usually is terminated at age 18.

Camp, ranch, or school programs are usually designed to provide juveniles with both academic and vocational skills as well as good work habits. Treatment is offered in the form of individual and family counseling, with an emphasis on building the minor's self-esteem and providing him or her with the coping skills needed to reintegrate with his or her family, or to be self-sufficient and emancipated.

Frequently, a camp or ranch commitment is the last effort by the court to utilize local resources in an effort to rehabilitate a minor; the disposition of last resort, before a commitment to the California Youth Authority. However, as we will discuss in a subsequent chapter, juvenile commitments to the state's institutional system is being phased out and will cease to exist by 2014. Counties will assume full responsibility for handling juvenile offenders.

Note that a commitment to **county jail is not an option** as a possible disposition (*In re* **Kirk G., 1977**; *In re* **Maria A., 1975**; and *In re* **Kenny A., 2000**). Occasionally, an individual may commit an offense at age 17 but turn age 18 before the dispositional hearing. He or she may be ordered to serve some time in juvenile hall as a condition of probation, and can even remain in juvenile hall through age 19, if so ordered. A minor age 16 or older may be ordered transferred from a juvenile hall to jail for detention purposes if a judge makes a special finding that the minor's behavior is too disruptive to the juvenile hall program. If confined in jail, the minor must be kept in quarters separate from adult prisoners.

Commitment to the State Division of Juvenile Facilities

The **Division of Juvenile Facilities (DJF)** is the state institutional system for juveniles. A minor is committed there either because he or she had received all the rehabilitative help that was available at the county level and had failed to reform (so the expression goes), or because the present offense and/or delinquent orientation of the minor posed a threat to the community and the minor was otherwise eligible for such a commitment.

This division (DJF) was an independent state agency once known as the California Youth Authority (CYA) until May 10, 2005, when it came under the newly created umbrella title, the Division of Juvenile Justice, which was placed within the California Department of Corrections and Rehabilitation. This change was a part of a SB 737, signed by Governor Schwarzenegger to reorganize the state's entire corrections system. The Department of Corrections was renamed the Department of Corrections and Rehabilitation under which is an adult services division and a juvenile justice division. Other agencies and boards had name changes to reflect an emphasis on rehabilitation.

This change also signaled the beginning of efforts to close down the juvenile institutional system and parole, except for the most serious offenders who could not be mixed with adults in a prison setting.

Today, the eligibility requirements for a court commitment to the DJF is clearly stated in Section 733, WIC. However, a ward of the juvenile court who meets any condition described below **shall not be committed** to the Division of Juvenile Facilities:

1. The ward is under 11 years of age.

2. The ward is suffering from any contagious, infectious, or other diseases that would probably endanger the lives or health of the other inmates of any facility.

3. The ward has been or is adjudged a ward of the court pursuant to Section 602, and the most recent offense alleged in any petition and admitted or found to be true by the court is not   described in subdivision (b) of Section 707, unless the offense is a sex offense set forth in subdivision (c) of Section 290.008 of the Penal Code.

Section 707b lists the most serious and violent offenses, and Section 290.008 lists the violent sex offenses. **Juveniles adjudicated a delinquent ward pursuant to Section 602 WIC shall now be retained at the county level for treatment, detention, and supervision.**

Deferred Entry of Judgment

Proposition 21 provides a procedure called **deferred entry of judgment** by which that adjudication/jurisdictional and disposition hearings are postponed pending the minor's success or failure to comply with the terms of this alternative program. If the minor qualifies and if the district attorney, defense attorney, and judge agree, the normal proceedings are postponed, during which time the minor is under the supervision of the probation officer for a period of between 12 and 36 months. To qualify for deferred judgment, all of the following circumstances must apply:

- the offense alleged is not one of those listed in §707(b) WIC
- the minor has not previously been committed to DJF/CYA
- the minor is at least 14 years of age at the time of the hearing
- the minor has not previously been declared a ward of the court for the commission of a felony offense
- the minor's record does not indicate that any prior probation was revoked for violating its terms and conditions

If the minor qualifies and all parties agree to using the deferred entry of judgment, the minor must admit the allegations of the petition and waive his or her right to a speedy hearing (trial), and agree to the terms and conditions that will be imposed during the period of supervision.

If the minor is granted deferred entry of judgment, the judge ...**shall impose**, as a condition of probation, the requirement that the minor be subject to warrantless searches of his or her person, residence, or property under his or her control, upon the request of a probation officer or peace officer. Other appropriate conditions will also be imposed.

Upon successful completion of the probation period the court will dismiss the petition and will deem that the arrest never occurred. The minor will not have a record. However, the record will be available upon any subsequent referral to court to use in determining if the minor qualifies for a second deferred judgment.

If the minor fails to comply with the terms and conditions of probation during the period of supervision he or she will be returned to court for an immediate pronouncement of judgment as a delinquent, and the matter will be scheduled for a dispositional hearing.

In addition to an immediate judgment upon a failure to comply, the minor may be found unfit as a juvenile if he or she commits two or more additional felonies during the period of supervision.

The benefits of using deferred entry of judgment are obvious. The minor is given the opportunity to prove himself or herself worthy to remain in the community, the minor avoids having a record, and everyone saves time, effort, and money spent by following the normal hearing process.

The Citation Hearing

The court proceedings described above apply to those minors actually delivered to probation by police. If a minor is merely cited, he or she must appear before a probation officer assigned as the Hearing Officer at a **citation hearing**. The procedures here are similar to those completed by Intake except that the focus is on what further action is necessary rather than the need to detain the minor.

The Hearing Officer may dismiss the matter or proceed under §654 WIC, with a period of informal supervision if the listed criteria are met. The officer may also request a petition if he or she thinks court action is necessary. The officer will be guided by the same factors that influence Intake in arriving at a decision as to what disposition would be appropriate. Since many juvenile cases are handled informally at the level of probation, without court action, it is less expensive for police to cite juveniles than to deliver them to a juvenile hall, and for probation to use the citation hearing process instead of the Intake/DA decision making procedures. Of course, it is even cheaper to divert the juvenile in the first place, than to cite or deliver him or her to the Hall.

Supplemental Petition Procedures

A supplemental petition is filed when a minor already is a ward of the court, and is alleged to have violated a condition of probation (§777 WIC). This petition is filed by the probation officer or district attorney if the violation does not amount to a new offense and by the DA if a new offense is alleged. When police deliver a minor to the Hall for a violation of probation, the officer would refer to this code section on the offense report. According to the code, the supplemental petition "shall contain a concise statement of facts sufficient to support the conclusion that the previous disposition has not been effective in the rehabilitation of the minor."

If the judge revokes probation, a new dispositional hearing is scheduled, and additional restrictions might be imposed. However, if the judge ordered a commitment to a county ranch or camp, at the original dispositional hearing, but suspended the execution of it pending the minor's successful completion of probation, the court need not hold another dispositional hearing. Of course, the offense cited in the original petition must meet the eligibility requirements listed above, if the minor is to be committed to DJF.

Under Proposition 21 guidelines it is sufficient for the court to find that the minor violated one of the conditions of probation. Then the court may order that the previous commitment be carried out (*In re* **Melvin J., 2000**).

Summary

This chapter detailed the bifurcated court hearing process: the adjudication/jurisdictional hearing and the dispositional hearing, along with the procedure known as deferred entry of judgment. Informal probation and citation hearings were discussed as well. The most commonly used dispositions were described. We noted that the purposes of juvenile court law attempt to blend the protection of the public with the care and treatment of the juveniles on the one hand, while attempting to hold the minor responsible for his or her conduct and administering some form of punishment.

In today's juvenile court, treatment and punishment are mixed haphazardly in a civil proceeding that has a strong overlay of criminal procedures. These inconsistencies and cross-purposes reflect a juvenile court system that is in transition from its past, but is not sure which direction to take to create its future. However, there is a definite movement away from committing juveniles to state supervision, and to keeping all but the most serious and violent offenders at the local level. The cost, of course, is shifting to the local level as well.

Case Decisions

In re Kenny A. (2000) HO 20202212

In re Kirk G. (1997) 67 CA. 3d 538

In re J. L. P. (1972) 25 CA 3d 86

In re Manuel L. (1993) 11 CA 4th 529

In re Maria A. (1975) 52 CA 3d 901

In re Melvin (2000) CA 4th 436

U.S. v. Juvenile Male (May 12, 2000) No. 99-30269, 9th CCP

Chapter 9: Probation Services

Key Terms and Concepts

Caseload assignment models
Court Investigation
Courtesy supervision
Division of Juvenile Facilities
Gang caseload
Geographic assignment model
Intake
Intensive supervision
Interstate Compact Agreement
Juvenile re-entry Grants
Luck of the Draw
Probation authority

Probation conditions
Probation intake
Probation investigation
Probation officer's role
Record sealing
Re-entry Dispositional Hearing
Regular supervision
Supervision model
Transfer of wardship
Violation/revocation procedures
Ward/wardship

Introduction

This chapter examines probation, its nature, scope, and purpose, and the roles of those who work within the system. In California probation is at the county level, which is not necessarily the case throughout the nation. The reader is referred back to Chapter 1, on the history of the California system for the relevant background.

Some of the roles and procedures of probation were detailed in previous chapters because juvenile probation is so closely aligned with the juvenile court, and with the pre-court process. Consequently, those roles and procedures will be touched on again only lightly, to place them within the total context of probation services. The main focus herein is the supervision of juvenile court wards, the legality of probation conditions, the requirements of violation/revocation procedures, and the possible consequences of succeeding or failing on probation.

The Organization of Probation Services

Probation was created by legislation in California in 1903. By 1905 probation was authorized to provide detention facilities, court reports, and case supervision. However, each county was left on its own to develop standards. By 1929 three counties still did not provide probation. And, it was not until after World War II that all the counties provided all of the services.

With one exception, the probation department of each county today comes within the legal authority of the juvenile court judge, a judge of the superior court. Each department has one chief probation officer and two work divisions, one for adult and one for juvenile services (if the department is large enough). Each division is administered by a director, appointed by the chief. The chief serves at the pleasure of the judge (although now in a few counties the board of supervisors has appointive authority), while the deputy probation officers usually have civil service protection. There can be frequent transfers of staff between divisions. Some staff views this as an opportunity for job enrichment or personal growth. However, in those departments in which the chief gives preference to one division over the other, a transfer might be seen as punishment for violating some bureaucratic rule.

The county San Francisco developed in a different organizational structure. They each formed two separate probation departments, with two chiefs, and provided little opportunity for the exchange of staff. Each department competed for budget resources with the Board of Supervisors.

Functional Specialization

The total work to be performed within an organization is divided into separate functions, or functional units. The typical organization has separate divisions, or work units responsible for Intake, court investigation, detention, placement, home supervision (for those pending court), and formal supervision (for wards on probation). Many of the larger departments within the state also might have specialized units that include the following: gang alternative diversion, gang suppression, school crime, electronic monitoring, drug testing, diversion, boot camp, transportation, electronic monitoring, and warrant and escape apprehension.

The size of a juvenile probation department will vary from county to county, according to the needs of delinquent populations and county budgets. As sizes vary, so do functions, roles, and job opportunities. Generally speaking, the smaller the county the more often a probation officer will be a generalist, performing a variety of functions. On the other hand, the larger the county, the more specialized the work roles become.

Job requirements and salaries also vary, with the larger and more affluent and concerned counties paying higher wages and providing more opportunities for job enrichment.

Authority of a Probation Officer

A county probation officer derives his or her authority from two sources. Section 283 of the W & I Code states simply that: "...probation officers...shall have the powers and authority conferred by law upon peace officers listed in Section 830.5 of the Penal Code."

Obviously, this referral means that both the status and authority of all probation officers, juvenile and adult, are conferred by the Penal Code. The section reads as follows:

> (Probation Officers) ... are peace officers whose authority extends to any place in the state while engaged in the performance of the duties of their respective employment, and for the purpose of carrying out the primary function of their employment....

The Penal Code extends and limits this authority as follows:

- to conditions of probation by any person in this state on probation
- to the escape of any inmate or ward from a state or local institution
- to the transportation of such persons
- to the rendering of mutual aid to any other law enforcement agency
- to violations of any penal provisions of law which are discovered while performing the usual or authorized duties of his or her employment

Probation Intake

The functions of an Intake probation officer were detailed in Chapter 7, and will not be presented here in any depth. By way of review, however, Intake screens the police reports and decides what further action is appropriate. If Intake believes that court action is warranted, he or she refers the case to the deputy district attorney assigned to juvenile court with a recommendation that a petition be filed. Intake also reviews the nature of the alleged offense and the minor's family and background to determine if detention in juvenile hall is necessary pending court action. Also, within the limits of §654 WIC, Intake may initiate a program of six months informal probation supervision for a juvenile. The reader is referred to the material presented in Chapter 7 if more details are needed.

Court Investigation

The function of the investigating officer was mentioned briefly in Chapter 7, but not described in any detail. When a juvenile case has been adjudicated and is set for a dispositional hearing, it is referred to the probation department's investigation unit. The supervisor logs it in and assigns it to one of the investigating officers to complete a social investigation and prepare the report for the court. Usually this assignment is made on the basis of whose turn it is, unless the department is large and has geographic assignments. Any one officer might prepare 20 to 25 of these reports a month.

This social investigation is a detailed examination of the minor's role in the offense, his or her prior delinquent history if any, and his or her social and family background. Statements of the victim, and the loss sustained by the victim are also included. The officer provides an assessment of why the minor got into trouble and what the court should order as a disposition to rehabilitate the minor and protect the community. If the officer recommends probation, he or she will suggest what conditions are relevant to the minor's supervision needs.

This investigation and report provide the primary basis for the court's disposition. The judge or referee will rely heavily on the expertise of the probation officer: on his or her investigative skills to ferret out the important data, on his or her capacity to assess the minor's problems and needs, and on his or her wisdom about what is best for the minor within the resources that are available.

The Supervision of Probation Cases

Probation, as a court status for juveniles, is defined as **the conditional, revocable, and supervised release of a ward into the community in lieu of commitment to an institution**. It gives the minor a chance to prove himself or herself worthy to remain within the community instead of being committed to a state institution. However, one unique feature of the juvenile system is that when a court declares a minor to be a ward of the court, that court retains jurisdiction on the minor until jurisdiction is terminated by the court, even if the minor is committed to a state institution.

The rehabilitation of juvenile offenders and the protection of the community are the goals of a supervising deputy probation officer. This dual role carries with it the two responsibilities of being a helper and an enforcer, which some say gives the probation officer a split personality. On the one hand he or she encourages the juvenile offender to participate with him or her in a relationship based on mutual respect, trust, rapport, confidence, and openness. On the other hand, the officer carries a badge and handcuffs, demands that the juvenile submit to random searches and chemical testing, and tells the juvenile that if he or she violates any orders given by the judge, he or she will be taken back to court and be held accountable.

Professional probation officers will use authority constructively to affect the growth and development of the juvenile, while at the same time protecting the community from any delinquent behavior. They will not be the type who needs to be liked so much that they cannot say "no", or the type whose source of satisfaction comes from wielding personal authority over others.

Most juveniles want and need limits, discipline, and accountability, as much as they need praise and support. In many cases, the parent/s of a juvenile court ward are either unwilling or unable to control and guide their children. Often, they wait until the child is 16 before they attempt to exercise any control, then wonder why the juvenile will not respond to them. Being a deputy probation officer is like being a super-parent. The officer really does sit in *loco parentis* and must constantly be available for each minor under his or her supervision to provide support, guidance, or discipline as the situation calls for it. How else can the officer show the juvenile that he or she cares?

The probation officer is not only the juvenile's caseworker and substitute parent, he or she is the role model for the juvenile. He or she represents the juvenile justice system to the minor and represents the type of person that the minor should emulate. Consequently, the officer should always be consistent, honest, and fair. The officer also should accept the minor as a valuable person, regardless of what the juvenile has done. What people do is not necessarily who they are. Juveniles do a lot of stupid, impulsive, immature, and illegal things while they are growing up. The officer, then, can judge of what a juvenile does, but not of what he or she is. That is not within the officer's role.

Caseload Size and Assignment Models

The **geographic model** is the most commonly used method of assigning cases for supervision. When juveniles come from court for probation supervision, they are referred to a field services division or unit for assignment to a caseload. Large departments have regional field offices in which the deputies supervise all the juveniles who reside within that region. In the small to medium sized counties the county itself is divided into areas of supervision according to the number of delinquents living there. In either event, an officer is, or officers are, assigned to supervise a caseload that is concentrated within a given geographic area.

This model offers several advantages. It limits the travel necessary for the officer. The supervising officer has the opportunity to learn the entire community within the area of supervision, which includes the schools served, businesses, community resources, and the population. The officer can also develop a network of contacts or information sources that facilitate the supervision of all the cases.

The **random assignment model**, sometimes referred to as the *numbers game*, might be used in small counties where the advantages of geographic assignment cited above either are not important or not considered. In this approach the supervisor of a field services unit keeps the number of cases supervised by each officer even, by assigning each ward referred by the court to the officer with the lowest number of cases. Assignment is based on which officer has the lowest caseload, and the purpose is to keep the workload evenly distributed.

The **special supervision/single factor model** is an approach in which all offenders with a special problem or need are assigned to one caseload. Examples of this include a caseload of heavy drug users, alcoholics, gang members, emotionally disturbed children, or placement cases. This model usually would fit the needs of the cases being supervised with the expertise of the officer, whereas the two other models described above would not.

The intensive **supervision model** is a caseload in which all the juveniles require very frequent contact and have special needs or problems. One type of intensive caseload that is commonplace in 2011, the **gang caseload**. Officers assigned to this type of supervision frequently are armed with a handgun, a vest, and handcuffs. They work regularly with local law enforcement in area sweeps, and searching offenders and their residences. The orientation in this type of supervision is much more of suppression and apprehension than it is rehabilitation. In some departments, this might not be a gang caseload, per se, but an **armed caseload**, in which officer supervise the full range of violent and dangerous offenders.

Regular Supervision

The ideal caseload size is approximately 50 regular cases; those without any unique problems or special supervision needs. This will allow the officer to visit with the juvenile approximately twice a month and to contact the parent/s and schools once per month. In reality caseload sizes range between 60 and 90, depending upon the county, and a supervising officer is usually expected to contact each ward, family, and school only once a month.

Frequently the officer on a regular supervision caseload classifies each case as to supervision needs when he or she receives the minor on probation. The officer might contact the minor once a week during the first month or so, then twice a month for the next month or so, then once a month or every other month thereafter, if all goes well. However, because controlling drug and gang activities are so much a part of today's supervision needs, it is seldom that all goes well. Much of the officer's time is spent running around his or her supervising area responding to one crisis after another; putting out brush fires, as it were, hoping that the whole forest does not go up in flames.

Conditions of Probation

Conditions of probation are actually orders mandated by the judge when he or she grants probation to the minor. They are designed to rehabilitate the minor and to protect the community from any further delinquent behavior by the minor. The W & I Code and the appellate court cases give the juvenile court wide latitude in ordering these conditions. The State has a responsibility (*parens patriae*) to provide the minor the guidance and direction he or she needs to grow into a responsible citizen.

On many occasions, the State's interest outweighs a juvenile's ordinary constitutional protections, and his or her conduct may be restricted to a greater degree than that of an adult. And, the court may consider not only the offense, but also the minor's entire social history (***In re* Todd L., 1981**; ***In re* Frankie J., 1988**; and ***In re* Tyrell J., 1994**). Section 727 WIC states that:

When a minor is adjudged a ward of the court on the grounds that he or she is a person described by...Section 602 **the court may make any and all reasonable orders** for the care, supervision, custody, conduct, maintenance, and support of the minor, including medical treatment, subject to further order of the court.

The court may make "**...any and all reasonable orders....**" This gives the court a great deal of authority, and only leaves room to argue over what is reasonable. Any orders made by the court are reasonable unless they bear no reasonable relationship to the underlying offense, social history, or future criminality (***In re* Gerald B., 1980**, and ***In re* Josh W., 1997**). Also, probation conditions must be "tailored carefully and reasonably related to the compelling state interests in reformation and rehabilitation" (***People v. Delvalle*, 1994**).

In a September 2000 case, ***In re* Antonio C.,** the Fifth DCA upheld the conditions that prohibited a minor from obtaining "...any new tattoos, brands, burns, piercings or any voluntary scarring," holding that these prohibitions were "...consistent with the reformative purposes of juvenile probation and constitute a reasonable exercise of the juvenile court's supervisory function to provide for the minor's safety and protection."

Probation conditions may not be vaguely worded. They must be stated in clear and definitive terms so that the juvenile knows what he or she may or may not do. In the case of ***In re* Sheena K., 2007**, the minor was placed on probation in 2002 and was ordered to not associate with anyone disapproved of by her probation officer. She apparently did, and was brought back to court for a probation violation. On appeal, the California Supreme Court ruled that the condition was unconstitutional and void-for-vagueness.

A probation condition "must be sufficiently precise for the probationer to know what is required of him, and for the court to determine whether the condition has been violated," if it is to withstand a challenge on the ground of vagueness. (***People v. Robertson* (1986) 178 Cal.App.3d at pp. 324-325.**) In the present case, the Court of Appeal concluded that the condition that defendant not associate with anyone "disapproved of by probation" was both vague and overbroad because the juvenile court did not require that in order to be in violation, defendant must know which persons were disapproved of by the probation officer. The court reasoned that "because of the breadth of the probation officer's power to virtually preclude the minor's association with anyone," defendant must be advised in advance whom she must avoid.

The decision was made to clarify the issue of vagueness and had no effect on Sheena K. because she died in 2006, at the age of 20 years.

In addition to being clearly stated and reasonable, the **minor must have the capacity** to comply with the condition. For example, *In re* **Robert M., 1985**, a 13-year-old boy, with an I.Q. of 70, was put on probation in Los Angeles County subject to the usual conditions, including that he attend a school program regularly and "…maintain satisfactory grades and citizenship." On two occasions, he received Ds and Fs on his report card, and was ordered to detention for 30 days by the court on each occasion for violating the conditions. Those decisions were appealed. The Second DCA ruled that it was beyond Robert's capacity to maintain satisfactory grades and citizenship and declared that portion of his probation order void.

Probation conditions fall into two categories: **standard conditions** are those required of all minors; and **special conditions** are those imposed selectively in certain situations as they relate to the offense and to the minor's particular rehabilitation needs. In some instances, the W & I Code is specific as to what conditions shall be imposed. For example, conditions that are often required include the following:

- that the minor attend an approved school program
- that the minor abide by a curfew
- that the minor submit to urine testing
- that the minor submit to a 3-way search clause
- that the minor participate in electronic monitoring
- that the parents or guardian participate with the minor in a counseling or education program

Juvenile Re-Entry Grants: the New Role for Juvenile Court and Probation

Before 2010, probation and parole supervision in California were separate entities, and never the twain shall meet, as it were. However, in mid-2010, counties began receiving youths discharged from DJF custody onto their probation caseloads, including those juveniles paroled before October 19, 2010. These juveniles would have been ineligible for a DJF commitment, under the new guidelines listed above on page 108. They come under juvenile court probation supervision.

In February 2011, counties began to receive all youths discharged from the Division of Juvenile Facilities (DJF) as a result of the **Juvenile Re-Entry Grant**, recently enacted by passage of AB 1628 (Chapter 729, Statutes of 2010).

The primary purpose of AB 1628 was to eliminate DJJ/DJF institutions and parole by July 2014, and shift this population to county supervision and aftercare. Funding provided via AB 1628 is intended to cover all local costs counties incur for the supervision of AB 1628 youths. Counties are prohibited from using AB 1628 funds to supplant existing funds. Furthermore, counties are required to provide evidence-based supervision and detention practices for those youths who come to them via AB 1628.

For **youths who are released from DJF custody** back to juvenile court, county probation departments generally receive $15,000 annually for the supervision and treatment of each youth for up to two years. After two years, the counties became responsible for the cost. For discharged youths who are transferred to a local juvenile facility for violating a condition of court-ordered supervision, counties receive $115,000 annually for each youth. (Refer to §731.1, 1719, 1766, 1767.35, 607.1, 1719.5, 1766.01 and 1767.36 WIC.)

The original committing court shall schedule a **re-entry dispositional hearing** in which the court will terminate the DJF's jurisdiction, and **will place the juvenile on county probation**, subject to the appropriate terms and conditions. The court's (probation) jurisdiction will terminate when the juvenile reaches age 25 years, or whenever the court feels that supervision is no longer needed.

This procedural change is so new that as of this writing, many probation officers and parole agents contacted by this writer did not know the complete details about how these procedures would be implemented. Indications are that most of these juveniles will be between the ages of 19 and 24 years at the time of their release. Nevertheless, they are still under the jurisdiction of the juvenile court. However, their actual supervision will be provided out of a probation department's adult division. And, any detention that is necessary will be provided in the local jail, not the juvenile hall.

Inter and Intra-state Transfer Cases

We live in a mobile society, and the parents of juvenile probation cases often relocate from the county of original jurisdiction. If the new address is within the state, and will be the permanent residence of a probationer, the legal jurisdiction of **wardship may be transferred** to the juvenile court in the new county of residence. This merely requires a verification of residence and the approval of the court in the new county.

If a minor moves to, or visits in, a new county on a temporary basis, the probation officer supervising the case may request the probation department in the new county to provide what is termed **courtesy supervision**. That is, the minor will be supervised and the minor is still obligated to comply with all the terms and conditions of probation. The reality is, however, that probation budgets are tight and resources are scarce. Each department is going to attend to its own cases first, placing courtesy supervision cases at the end of a long priority list.

Courtesy supervision may be requested and provided by probation departments, and parole agencies for that matter, within different states by an arrangement in which they participate, known as **The Interstate Compact Agreement on Juveniles**. This agreement is administered by staff in an office in Sacramento. When a juvenile relocates to a new state, the sending state (original state) forwards copies of the legal documents and probation (or parole) orders to the Interstate Compact Office. Staff there forward the papers and request supervision from the office located closest to the juvenile's new residence. A probation officer there provides the required supervision.

Each state participating in this agreement also must designate one of its institutions as a Compact Institution in which a juvenile may be detained for any lawful purpose by the authority of the original probation officer.

Termination of Wardship and Probation

One of the many oddities in juvenile procedures is the fact that a person must commit an offense while under the age of 18 years in order to come within the jurisdiction of the juvenile court. However, once a minor has been declared a ward, the court may retain jurisdiction until the minor reaches age 21 years, or even age 25, depending upon the situation. However, if a ward between the ages of 18 and 21 years commits a new offense, he or she undoubtedly will be charged with a crime by the district attorney, and will face criminal proceedings in adult court, because he or she is beyond the jurisdiction of the juvenile court for any new offense. This is just another inconsistency within the juvenile justice system. Wardship may be terminated by the juvenile court at any time the court thinks it is in the best interests of the minor and public safety.

A parent or guardian or the minor may also petition the court to terminate jurisdiction or to change any court orders as well. However, any change or termination is at the discretion of the court. As a rule of thumb a supervising probation officer will advise a juvenile at the time probation is granted that if all goes well and the minor complies with the terms of probation for one year the officer will return the case to court with a recommendation for termination of wardship. If problems develop within the year, the officer may continue supervision until he or she thinks that probation is no longer necessary.

Sealing of Records

A juvenile may have his or her delinquent (not traffic) record sealed after termination of wardship upon reaching age 18 years, or five years after the termination, whichever occurs first. However, the juvenile has the responsibility to petition the court to seal the record. It is not done automatically. If the juvenile does not initiate the sealing, the record will remain open. Usually, the probation officer that supervised the juvenile petitions the court on the minor's behalf and completes the sealing process.

The name *sealing* comes from the old practice of placing a juvenile's complete record in a large envelope and actually sealing it with a large blob of sealing wax, in which the county seal was then embossed.

Before issuing a sealing order, the court must be satisfied that the minor "...has not been convicted of a felony or a misdemeanor involving moral turpitude and that rehabilitation has been attained." The court shall order all records sealed and shall deem that the arrest never occurred. Also, in any case in which a ward was required to register as a sex offender pursuant to Section 290 PC, the court shall provide in its sealing order that the juvenile is relieved from that registration requirement.

However, notwithstanding any other provision of law, the court shall not order the person's records sealed in any case in which the person has been found by the juvenile court to have committed an offense listed in subdivision (b) of Section 707 when he or she had attained 14 years of age or older.

A juvenile delinquent adjudication and disposition in a prior (violent felony) case does not result in the accused of having been convicted of a serious felony for purposes of PC §12201.1, subdivision (b) (1) ...An order adjudicating a minor to be a ward of the juvenile court shall not be deemed a criminal conviction of a criminal for any purpose, nor shall proceedings in the juvenile court be deemed a criminal proceeding.

Once a record is sealed, only the minor can petition the court to re-open the record. See Senate Bills 312, 393, and 529 for more details on sealing of records after 2018.

Violations and Revocation of Probation

A minor may be found in violation of probation for either committing a **new offense** or for not complying with a condition of probation, termed a **technical violation**. In either event, the supervising probation officer often has wide discretion in deciding whether to allege a probation violation. Instead of taking formal action, the officer may admonish and counsel the minor. However, if a new offense is serious, or if the technical violations become repetitive, the officer will refer the case back to court by filing a **supplemental petition**.

A supplemental petition is filed with the court by probation or the DA under §777 WIC alleging the violation, and describing the facts that support the allegation. If the violation is for a new offense, only the district attorney has the legal authority to file.

The legal requirements that must be met in a supplemental §777 petition depend upon what the probation officer recommends as the new disposition. If the recommendation is that the minor be removed from the physical custody of his or her parents and placed elsewhere or committed to a state institution, or to a county facility for a period longer than 30 days, the petition must contain facts to support the allegation that the previous disposition "...has not been effective in the rehabilitation or protection of the minor." (*In re* **Martin L., 1986**; *In re* **James S., 1978**). The court also must make a finding to that same effect.

If the recommendation and court finding includes a commitment to a county facility for 30 days or less, it is not necessary to allege and prove the ineffectiveness of a previous disposition. However, before any commitment is ordered to exceed 15 days the court must determine and consider what effect the commitment would have on the minor's schooling or current employment. The court may not make any such commitment order more than twice during a period of wardship.

In any violation hearing a minor is guaranteed all the due process (***Gagnon V. Scarpelli*, 1973**; *In re* **Francis W., 1974**) that he or she could expect in any original proceeding except that the allegation need only be proven by a **preponderance of the evidence** (*In re* **Glen J., 1979**), rather than beyond a reasonable doubt.

Most violation of probation hearings do not result in the minor's probation being revoked. Rather, the conditions are modified in some fashion to help in the court's efforts to rehabilitate the minor. These modifications could include a short period of detention in juvenile hall or a commitment to some county ranch, school, camp, or juvenile hall rehabilitation program. Revocation is the choice of last resort, when all else fails. When the court believes that the minor is no longer amenable to the rehabilitative treatment available at the county level and/or "…poses a significant risk to the community, the court will revoke probation and commit the minor to the California Division of Juvenile Facilities (DJF).

Also, the minor must meet the eligibility requirements by committing one of the listed 707bWIC or 290 PC offenses. This type of commitment is, however, is in a state of flux, and may no longer be available in the near future.

Another oddity of juvenile procedures is that if the court commits a minor to DJF, it set what is known as the maximum confinement time that the ward may serve, using the determinant sentencing times for crimes provided in the Penal Code. Along with that oddity, is another feature of the new parole release and supervision model described above. If one of the juveniles referred by DJF back to court for probation supervision instead of release on parole is taken into custody on a probation violation, and the juvenile court finds that a juvenile is, in fact, in violation of his or her release conditions, he or she cannot be returned to DJF. If any sentence time is forthcoming as a result of the violation, it will be served in the local jail. And any time given must be added to the time the juvenile already spent in a DJF Facility and the total time may not exceed the maximum confinement time originally given by the court.

Summary

Many juveniles never reach the formal justice system. They are diverted by police into one of the many education, training, or treatment programs available throughout the state. Another portion of the juvenile population never gets caught. They engage in a variety of delinquent activities, usually on an experimental basis, during their formative years, but grow up to become productive members of the community.

Those juveniles who do get caught and who are not diverted frequently end up as a part of the juvenile court's probation system. This chapter examined probation, its nature, scope, and purpose, and the roles of those who work within the system. The main focus herein was the supervision of juvenile court wards, the legality of probation conditions, the requirements of violation/revocation procedures, and the possible consequences of succeeding or failing on probation, probation violation and commitment, or honorable discharge and record sealing.

The majority of probationers either complete probation honorably and have wardship terminated or their wardship is terminated for them when they reach age 18 years. The vast majority of juveniles are handled at the county level, either with probation services in the community or in one of the many county ranches, camps, or schools. As we shall see in the subsequent chapter, probation departments have now taken on the additional responsibility of supervising juveniles released from state institutions.

Case Decisions

Gagnon v. Scarpelli (1973) 411 U.S. 778

In re Antonio C. (2000) CA 4th

In re Francis W. (1974) 42 CA. 3d 892

In re Frankie J. (1988) 198 CA 3d 1149; 244 Cal. Rptr. 254

In re Gerald B. (1980) 105 CA 3d 119

In re Glen J. (1979) 97 CA 3d 891

In re James S. (1978) 81 CA 3d 198; 144 Cal. Rptr. 893

In re Josh W. (1997) 55 CA 4th 1

In re Martin L. (1986) 187 CA 3d 534; 232 Cal. Rptr. 43

In re Robert M. (1985) 163 CA 3d 812; 209 Cal. Rptr. 657

In re Sheena K (2007) 116 CA 4th 436

In re Todd L. (1981) 113 CA 3d 14; 169 Cal. Rptr. 625

In re Tyrell J. (1994) 8 CA 4th 68

People v. Delvalle (1994) 26 CA 4th 869

People v. Westbrook (2002) CA 4th 14

Chapter 10: The Division of Juvenile Facilities

Key Terms and Concepts

AB 1628
Board Confinement Time
California Youth Authority
Court commitment time
Division of Juvenile Facilities
Division of Juvenile Justice
Electronically Enhanced
Honorable discharge
Institutions
Intensive Re-entry
Interstate Compact Agreement
Juvenile Parole Board

Maximum confinement time
Parole
Parole agent
Parole consideration date
Parolee
Parole discharge date
Parole release date
Probation Referral
Reception center
Re-entry dispositional hearing
Violation/revocation procedures

Introduction

This chapter focuses entirely on the **Division of Juvenile Facilities (DJF)**. As we mentioned in the previous chapter, it is the state organization that administers the institutional services for young offenders, and was known for years as the California Youth Authority (CYA). See the *Preface* for details. It is similar to the prison services given adults committed to the California Department of Corrections and Rehabilitation (CDCR). The DJF offers an array of institutional services and programs. The purpose of DJF is reflected in its mission statement:

> The Mission of the DJF is to protect society from the consequences of criminal activity and to that purpose community restoration, victim restoration, and offender training and treatment shall be substituted for retributive punishment and shall be directed toward the correction and rehabilitation of young persons who have committed public offenses.

Protection of society is the agency's primary purpose, although that protection is to be accomplished through rehabilitative services for youthful offenders. DJF also is heavily involved in providing delinquency prevention programs throughout the state, and in assisting local agencies with resources and training. Before we examine the current services provided by DJF, we will first review the history of that agency's development under the former name, CYA.

A Brief History of the Division of Juvenile Facilities

The organization established as the state's juvenile institutional system was first named the California Youth Authority (CYA) and was established by law in 1941, to accept all court commitments under the age of 23 years. In 1943, the Governor transferred to CYA the management of California's existing reform schools: Preston School of Industry in Ione, the Whittier School for Boys (re-named the Fred C. Nelles School for Boys), and the Ventura School for Girls. The total ward population at the time was 1,080 in the institutions and 1,625 on parole.

Over the years, CYA grew considerably larger. In 1943, it transferred 50 boys from various county jails to the Calaveras Big Tree Park, where they built a 100-bed camp. In that same year, CYA purchased the Knights of Pythias Old Peoples' Home and Orphanage off Highway 12, in rural Sonoma County, renovated the grounds and buildings, and opened the Los Guilicos School for Girls. Fricot Ranch School, a camp-like setting for young boys in the Sierra foothills, opened in 1944. These facilities were insufficient to house all the young commitments awaiting delivery to CYA. Many were detained in local juvenile halls, county jails, and on two army bases. Over-crowding was as much a problem then as now.

At the close of World War II, the army camps were closed, and the need for new facilities reached the crisis stage. The Legislature responded by authorizing additional institutions. The California Vocation Institution at Lancaster was opened for older boys in 1945. Pine Grove Camp also opened in 1945, and Camp Ben Lomond opened in 1947. Also, in 1947, the Paso Robles School for Boys opened on a 200-acre abandoned army base with 40 barracks.

Commitments to CYA continued to increase. In 1954, a **reception center** and clinic was opened in Perkins (now a part of Sacramento) in the northern part of the state, and at Norwalk in the south. Mt. Bullion Camp opened in 1956 near Mariposa; the

Youth Training Center (YTC) opened in Ontario in 1960; and Washington Ridge Camp near Nevada City opened in 1961. Additional camps were opened in 1972 and 1979.

The California Youth Authority was given departmental status in 1953, and in 1961, it became a part of the state's Youth and Adult Corrections Agency, along with CDC.

In 1964, a reception center and clinic for girls was opened at the Ventura School, leaving the Norwalk Clinic exclusively for boys. The Northern California Youth Center opened in 1965, on the southern edge of Stockton. The original plans called for twelve 400-bed facilities clustered around an administrative center. Each facility was to have dorm-style living for 50 boys in each wing of four two-wing units, with the wings separated by a staff office.

Only four of the planned facilities were opened: O. H. Close School for Boys in 1966; Karl Holton School for Boys in 1967; Dewitt Nelson School for Boys in 1971; and the N. A. Chaderjian School in 1991.

Housing in the first three institutions was of the dorm-style, reflecting an open environment, while that of the Chaderjian School uses the so-called **270° plan**, in which large square housing buildings are divided inside into two or more quads by walls. Supervising staff sat in a tower-like room positioned above the quads, giving them 270 degrees of vision, while the cell-like rooms ringed the perimeter of each quad. Other staff worked on the floors below.

The growth of CYA's population slowed, and even declined, in the late 1960s and 1970s, with the implementation of a probation subsidy program and the law change eliminating the juveniles committed for status offenses. In fact, several institutions, such as the Fricot School and Los Guilicos School, were closed and sold when it appeared that California had found the magic solution to treating delinquents. However, Institutions were expanded and new ones built in the 1970's, with the Herman G. Stark Youth Training School (discussed below) in Chino and the above-mentioned Chaderjian Correctional Facility in Stockton, among the most recently built.

On May 10, 2005, CYA, as an organization, was re-named the **Division of Juvenile Facilities** and it came under the newly created umbrella title of the **Division of Juvenile Justice**, which was placed as the juvenile wing under the California Department of Corrections and Rehabilitation. This change was a part of a SB 737 signed by Governor Schwarzenegger to reorganize the state's entire corrections system. The Department of Corrections was renamed as the Department of Corrections and Rehabilitation under which are an adult services division and a juvenile justice division. Other agencies and boards had name changes to reflect an emphasis on rehabilitation. Names were changed but individuals in those agencies and boards remained the same. After 2014, however, little remained of the state's role in juvenile justice.

As of January 2017, only the following juvenile facilities remain open: Ventura Youth Correctional Facility, N.A. Chaderjian School, O. H. Close, and Pine Grove Youth Conservation Center. The other facilities have been reassigned as institutions for adult offenders.

DJF's Population Profile and Cost

DJF once operated the largest youthful offender program in the nation, and probably in the world. Today, it is but a shell of its former self, and it seems to be shrinking as I write. The designed bed capacity for all the institutions combined was 6,266. By 1996, the actual capacity was 10,122, but it has declined rapidly, given the state's efforts to trim the budget and to move the responsibility for treating juveniles back to local jurisdictions. It was costing approximately $255,000 per ward, per year, to house juveniles, and the success of the DJF's programs was questioned by many. As of May 2016, the number of juveniles detained had reached 679; 26 of which were female, 636 were juvenile males, and 17 were male adult court commitments.

As of June 2018, there were a total of 629 residents; 580 were juvenile court commitments and 49 were commitments from criminal courts.

DJF Programs

DJF once operated eleven institutions and four camps which provided a wide array of rehabilitation programs. Two institution-based camps, Los Robles at El Paso de Robles (Paso Robles), and the Carraway Fire and Public Service Camp in Stockton, provided extensive training for males in fighting forest fires and doing soil and forest conservation work. The Ventura (School for Girls) Youth Correctional Facility provides similar training for females. Wards were also trained in fire-fighting and soil/forest conservation at the Preston and H. M. Stark institutions.

It is interesting to note that in the 2000 edition of this text, all the Youth Authority institutions were named *Schools*. Four years later, many have been re-named a Correctional *Facility*. In the 1970s and '80s, and even into the '90s, staff at the schools wore casual civilian dress. Later, special security staff wore blue blazers, and were separate from other staff. Now, one sees staff wearing uniforms and what looks like army fatigues, carrying mace, and wearing knife-proof vests. These changes reflect both an orientation away from treatment toward confinement, and the changing and more violent-prone nature of juveniles committed there.

W & I Code §1250 was amended effective in 2004 to establish the Heman G. Stark Youth Training School for the confinement of juvenile males convicted as adults in criminal court. Now it is one of several former DJF facilities used for the adult population.

It is beyond the scope and purpose of this book to enumerate the current programs one might now find within the DJF facilities. If they were listed, they probably would be changed by the time this book came into use.

The Juvenile Parole Board

The juvenile parole board is often referred to as just the parole board. It was first established as the Youthful Offender Parole Board by the Legislature in 1941, as a part of the California Youth Authority. However, it was separated from CYA as a separate entity in 1980. It had a 7-member Board, whose members were appointed by the Governor and confirmed, first by the Senate Rules Committee, then by the full Senate.

As of 2004, §716 WIC was amended abolishing this Board, and established the Youth Authority Board, whose membership consisted of the same members who were on the Board just abolished. However, effective, July 1, 2005, the Youth Authority Board was abolished, as were the adult parole board, and a single state parole board was established called the **Board of Parole Hearings.** It is a 17-member board appointed by the Governor and confirmed by the Senate. Twelve members hear adult parole cases and **five hear juvenile parole cases.** The juvenile board is now known as the **Juvenile Parole Board (JPB)**. Names were changed, but the players remained the same.

As of this writing, the board is called The Board of Juvenile Hearings. Its staff includes an executive officer and three commissioners, appointed by the governor for terms of four years. There are also civil service hearing officers and administrative staff.

The Board of Juvenile Hearings (Board) conducts a number of hearings with youth under the jurisdiction of the Division of Juvenile Justice (DJJ). These hearings include:

- Initial Case Reviews, held within 45 days of a youth's arrival in DJJ;
- Annual Case Reviews, a yearly check-in on a youth's progress;
- Discharge Consideration Hearings, to determine whether a youth is ready for release from DJJ to county probation supervision; and
- Honorable Discharge Hearings to former DJJ youth who have completed probation and been in the community for at least 18 months.

The Board's Authority

Although considered a parole board, the range of the Board's authority over what happens to a juvenile committed to DJF was far more comprehensive than that implied in the mere name *parole*. Their control was almost total. In this area of examination, it operates far differently than the parole board members hearing adult cases.

Before 2011, when a minor was committed to DJF, the Board had the authority to:

1. accept or reject the minor and may return him or her to court
2. determine the length of confinement
3. order the place of confinement
4. order the type of programming for each minor
5. determine how often a minor will appear before the Board for parole consideration, and when the minor is actually ready for release
6. order parole
7. set parole conditions
8. revoke or modify parole
9. discharge a juvenile parolee from parole

As of 2011, items 6 through 9 were no longer within the scope of the Board's authority. This was a significant change in juvenile procedures, and the year 2011, will become the benchmark used to measure the rise and demise of DJJ and DJF. This change is detailed below under the section, *Parole Consideration*. **Juvenile parole was abolished completely in July 2014.** All aftercare supervision in by probation.

The Purposes of a DJF Commitment

Prior to 1984, both the Legislature and the courts held that "...juvenile commitment proceedings are designed for the purpose of rehabilitation and treatment, not punishment (***In re* Aline D., 1975**)." A commitment to CYA was appropriate "...only in the most serious cases after all else has failed (***In re* Eugene R., 1980**)"; and it had to be "...supported by substantial evidence on the record that the minor would benefit from the training and treatment in CYA (***In re* Aline D., 1975**)", and that "...a less restrictive alternative would be ineffective (***In re* Ricky H., 1981**)."

In 1984, the Legislature modified the purpose of juvenile court law "...to provide for the protection and safety of the public...." The California Supreme Court has supported this blending of public safety and protection with the treatment of the minor (***In re* Lawanda L., 1986**). Consequently, a commitment to DJF often combines the court's concern for the minor's rehabilitation with the application of punishment in the form of time served, and the need to protect the public by removing the minor from the community.

This blending might seem like the Legislature and court are working at cross purposes by attempting to treat, punish, and protect at the same time. Actually, it reflects the nature of the juvenile justice system in transition from a protection and treatment model to the justice model; from individualized treatment to generalized punishment.

The DJF Commitment: Calculating the Commitment Time

This shift from treatment to punishment is evident in the way the court's authority has changed in recent years. Before 1982 a minor could be committed to a local ranch or camp, or to DJF for an indefinite period, up to the age at which legal jurisdiction would end, age 21 years, or in some cases, age 25. Now, however, a juvenile may not receive more commitment time in any type of secure facility than an adult could receive as a criminal sentence, regardless of the minor's treatment needs (see, ***In re* Bryant R., 2003**). This limits misdemeanor commitments to either six months or one year, and felony commitments to whatever time the Penal Code provides for adult sentences.

The Welfare and Institutions Code authorizes a judge to commit a minor to DJF, as we have noted, but the juvenile law does not provide any time frame for such a commitment other than the maximum jurisdictional age. Therefore, when a judge commits a minor to DJF for *rehabilitation*, he or she must refer to the Penal Code and follow the sentencing procedures and guidelines of the adult **Determinate Sentence Law (DSL)** established by the Legislature, as provided in Penal Code Section 1170.

Under the adult DSL, every felony carries three possible prison terms: the **presumptive term (middle), the mitigated term (lower), and the aggravated term (upper).** The judge considers all factors in mitigation and aggravation, and may then impose whichever term he or she thinks is appropriate. However, the judge may not choose the aggravated term unless all the factors in aggravation were either admitted or proven in court. The judge may also add on time for the sentence **enhancements**, listed in the Penal Code, which have been alleged and proven in court. In multiple offense cases the judge also must order whether the terms are to be served consecutively or concurrently.

The Legislature imposed these same adult sentencing procedures in juvenile court proceedings. The juvenile court judge refers to the Penal Code and selects one of the three adult terms. If there are multiple offenses, the judge picks one-third the middle term for all but the most serious offense, which receives the full term. This sets the **maximum confinement time** that a juvenile may be detained in DJF for treatment. In fact, it is the maximum combined time the juvenile may be detained anywhere. The same procedure applies in adult court for committing the young adult convicted of a crime.

The inconsistency by the Legislature in applying an adult sentencing scheme to juvenile treatment goals is made more obvious when one notes that in determining these adult times for felonies, Penal Code Section 1170(a)(1) states in absolute terms that: "...the purpose of imprisonment for crime is punishment. This purpose is best served by terms proportionate to the seriousness of the offense..."

The Legislature has imposed an adult punishment model of sentencing on a juvenile system, which still perceives that its primary responsibility is rehabilitation. On the other hand, the Legislature has provided commitment time guidelines for juveniles in a separate code that the Board should follow, rather than actually following the commitment time given by the judge. In other words, the time given a minor is binding on the minor, but DJF is not bound to keep the minor that entire time. The Juvenile Board decides how much time the minor will actually serve.

Regardless of age, offense, or violence potential, §731 WIC provides that a minor may not be held in physical confinement for a period of time in excess of the maximum term set by the court.

On January 22, 2007, the U. S. Supreme Court held that the portion of California's DSL which allowed judges to choose the aggravated term for adults, based on factors not found true by a jury, is unconstitutional. That decision does not apply in juvenile court because juries are not used in juvenile court in California. Consequently, the judge hears and considers those factors in mitigation and aggravation, while hearing all the evidence in the adjudication hearing.

The DJF Commitment: The Board Confinement Time

When a minor is committed to DJF, he or she is sent initially to a Reception Center at Norwalk, or Ventura, where he or she undergoes a 45 to 60-day period of diagnostic study and evaluation. This includes educational and psychological testing, medical and dental examinations, and an assessment of the minor's background and treatment needs. A report is prepared, with a recommendation to the Board as to what programming would benefit the minor. The Board then meets as a Panel Board, reviews the evaluation report, and decides whether the minor can benefit from the rehabilitative programs available at DJF.

If the Juvenile Parole Board thinks that the minor cannot benefit from a DJF program, the Board can refuse to accept the commitment and return the minor to the court for another disposition. The Board can also refuse anyone with a communicable disease, or one whose behavior would be disruptive to a DJF program. Also, there are certain felonies, as defined in Penal Code Section 1192.7, which disqualify a youth from receiving a DJF commitment. If the Board accepts the commitment, it sets a **release consideration date (RCD)** for the minor, derived from an **offense baseline chart**.

Programming and Review

After the juvenile's RCD has been determined, the Board decides in which institution the minor will program, and in what program the juvenile will participate, ie., school, vocational training, or a forestry camp.

The case of each ward is reviewed annually by a Panel Board to determine how the minor is programming and/or if the initial time set by the Board should be modified with a new RCD. Now, the Parole Board may deviate in time up to six months. In addition, if the minor acts out within the institution, a disciplinary hearing may be conducted by a Board member or civil service Referee, who can add up to six months' time to the RCD. If the case is referred up to a Full Board *en banc* it has no limit on the amount of time it may deviate. It may release immediately or detain until the maximum confinement time is served.

When a ward completes his or her Board-ordered confinement time, he or she appears before a Full Board, who meets at the institution to determine if the minor is ready for release. The Board may deny release and continue the case for up to one year, with a new RCD. The Board may continue a case like this for good cause, denying parole until the juvenile either serves all of the maximum confinement time given by the judge, or reaches the age at which jurisdiction terminates.

Rarely does a juvenile serve his or her entire maximum confinement time. Usually the Board grants discharge when and if a ward satisfactorily completes the Board's ordered time and the program.

Discharge (Parole) Consideration

Juvenile parole, as we know it, is now a misnomer (AB 1628). As was stated in the previous chapter, post-release will be by the county probation department. Effective January 17, 2011, the Juvenile Parole Board was no longer authorized to release wards on parole. Instead, the Board now refers the cases of juveniles ready for **discharge** from DJF to the **committing court**, 60 days prior to the release date, along with the Board's post-release recommendations as to what conditions it suggests for effective supervision. The committing court will schedule a **re-entry dispositional hearing** and will refer the case to the **probation investigation** unit to prepare a court report as to the appropriate supervision terms and conditions. **The juvenile will subsequently be placed on probation by the Court**.

As of July 1, 2014, all juvenile parolees were transferred to the committing juvenile court jurisdictions for probation supervision.

The new release and discharge to probation supervision was detailed in Section 1768.01 WIC. It requires DJF, at least 60 days before a ward's scheduled discharge consideration hearing before the Board, to provide the original committing court and the probation department with the most recent written case review, as well as notice of the **discharge consideration hearing date**.

At the discharge consideration hearing, the Board considers everything documented in the minor's file, to include school or vocational trade reports, behavior, staff reports, and any diagnostic reports that might be available. This information usually is provided in a cumulative report, prepared by an institutional parole agent or counselor. If all is favorable, a release and discharge to probation supervision date is scheduled for the juvenile. The Board then must send its post-release recommendations about the juvenile's supervision needs to the court, within seven days, and set a specific release date at least fourteen days after that determination.

Section 1766.01(c)(6) WIC requires the committing court to hold a **re-entry disposition hearing** to determine and set the appropriate terms and conditions for the juvenile's probation supervision. The court will include any recommendations by the Board that the court deems appropriate for the best interests of the minor and the public safety.

Since there are less than 700 juvenile court ward commitments in DJF at this time, their releases to the various counties will probably have a minimum impact on their resources.

Division of Parole Operations

Parole services were operated by the Division of Juvenile Parole Operations, which made them agents of the Executive branch of government. Parole agents worked in this division, however, they also were accountable to the Board of Parole Hearings for the supervision provided parolees, and they were the enforcement arm of the state parole system to make sure the parolees obey the conditions.

This Division was phased out of existence in 2014, when all after-care supervision was returned to the county level.

Reduction of Time to Serve

Proposition 47, passed by the voters in November 2014, re-classified certain no serious, nonviolent offenses from felonies to misdemeanors. Proposition 47 also enacted a statute (§ 1170.18 P.C.) that permits offenders to petition the superior court to re-designate their felony convictions and reduce their sentences based on the new misdemeanor classification. This same procedure was made applicable for juveniles wanting to reduce the classification of their offense designations from felony to misdemeanor, thereby lessening the confinement time that may be served (***Alejandro N. v. Superior Court*, 2015**).

Summary

This chapter focused entirely on the Division of Juvenile Facilities, once known and often still called the California Youth Authority (CYA). DJF is the state organization that administers the institutions and parole services for young offenders. The array of institutional services and programs were mentioned, but not detailed because they frequently change. The roles and functions of the Board of Parole Hearings were examined as well.

It was noted that the Board is the primary controlling authority for all activities, programs, and commitment time experienced by the wards. However, their authority to arrange for supervision has shifted to the wards' committing courts and probation services. AB 1628 has reorganized the entire juvenile institutional and parole system.

Internet References

http://www.cdcr.ca.gov/Juvenile_Justice/index.html

http://www.cdcr.ca.gov/

http://www.cya.ca.gov/

http://www.topjuveniledefender.com/california_youth_authority.html

http://www.populationconnection.org/239/project.html?id=92

http://www.nicic.org/Library/020367

Case Decisions

In re Alejandro N. v. Superior Court (2015), No. D067445 Cal.App.4th

In re Aline D. (1975) 14 Cal 3d 557

In re Bryant R., (2003) CA 4th (No. F041423)

In re Eugene R. (1980) 107 CA 3d 617

In re Lawanda L. (1986) 178 CA 3d 423

In re Ricky H. (1981) 30 Cal 3d 176

Morrissey v. Brewer (1972) 408 U.S. 471

Chapter 11: The Dependent Child: Physical and Emotional Abuse

Key Terms and Concepts

Check the welfare
Child abuse
Child Protective Services
Consequence of abuse
Corporal punishment
Dependent child
Dependent Unit/Children's shelter
Dysfunctional family
Emotional assault

Emotional deprivation
Emotional maltreatment
Failure to thrive syndrome
General neglect
Indicators of abuse
Parenting skills
Physical assault
Physical neglect
Protective custody
Severe neglect

Introduction

This chapter is about a sordid subject, child abuse. It deals specifically with the physical and emotional abuse of children. It is the most deplorable of all crimes and has an impact upon the victim, and upon society, that is more devastating than any other type of offense.

Thousands of children are abused and/or killed every year, usually in their home and usually by someone who is responsible for their care. In fact, child abuse is the leading cause of death among children under four years of age. The number of reported cases of abuse is on the increase. This increase might be the result of an actual increase in the number of children who are abused or it might be that more cases are reported. In either event, the trend is alarming. In Chapters 2 and 3 we examined procedures for the status offender, the 601, a juvenile who violated a law once created just for his or her age status.

In Chapter 4, we learned about the delinquent, a juvenile who violated Section 602 WIC, in that he or she committed some act prohibited by a statutory law, such as those described in the Penal Code or Health and Safety Code. In those instances, we focused on the juvenile as the offender, and it was his or her acting out that brought him or her within the jurisdiction of the juvenile court.

Our focus must now shift from viewing the juvenile as an offender to considering him or her as the victim. The neglected or abused child has done nothing wrong. Rather, he or she has been victimized by an act or omission of another, usually a parent or caretaker. Under these circumstances the abused child comes within the jurisdiction of the juvenile court under **Section 300 WIC**, which is detailed below. This jurisdiction reflects the concept of ***parens patriae*** at its finest, because the only concern of the juvenile court in §300 cases is the protection and welfare of the child who cannot protect himself or herself.

Much of the material in this chapter deals with a series of sections in the W & I Code that begin with 300 as they relate to the procedures for law enforcement, the courts, and aftercare services. However, in every abuse situation that brings the child within the description of 300 WIC, we also have a violation of a criminal code that brings an adult within the description of a criminal code section. Consequently, we have a parallel series of Penal Code sections to study, as they describe the adult conduct that caused the abuse.

We begin this chapter with a shortened version of Section 300 WIC. The section is long and complex and it is hoped that this shortened version will be more readable and will serve as a bridge to a later reading of the full code section.

This is followed by the description of the legal authority given to law enforcement to intervene by §305 WIC and the options and discretion an officer has after exercising his or her authority to intervene by §307 WIC. Next, we categorize abuse into four types; three of which are the subjects of this chapter. Each type will be presented separately, first with its legal definition, then with a description of how and/or why each type of abuse occurs. Also included is a summary of the Penal Code sections that apply in each case as well as the procedures a police officer should follow when called to investigate and resolve each type of abuse situation. The consequences of abuse are stated as well. Following this the child abuse reporting laws are reviewed as to what must be reported and by whom these reports must be made.

The Dependent Child and Police Authority

The Dependent Child

The full legal description of the dependent child - that is, one who comes within the description of Section 300 WIC - is lengthy and complex. It contains ten subsections, plus a narrative stating the intent of the Legislature when the law was enacted. As stated above, what follows is a shortened version of those subsections.

The W & I Code states that any minor who comes within any of the following descriptions is within the jurisdiction of the juvenile court which may adjudge that person to be a dependent child of the court. These conditions are what a law enforcement officer, probation officer, or social worker look for in determining if abuse is occurring or has occurred and if the minor should be taken into protective custody

- the minor has suffered, or there is a substantial risk that the minor will suffer, serious physical harm inflicted **non-accidentally** upon the minor by the minor's parents or guardian
- the minor has suffered, or there is a substantial risk that the minor will suffer, serious physical harm or illness, as a result of the failure or inability of his or her parent or guardian to adequately supervise or protect the minor
- the willful or negligent failure of the minor's parents or guardian to adequately supervise or protect the minor from the conduct of the custodian with whom the minor has been left

- the willful or negligent failure of the parent or guardian to provide the minor with adequate food, clothing, shelter, or medical treatment, or by the inability of the parent or guardian to provide regular care for the minor due to the parent's or guardian's mental illness, developmental disability, or substance abuse

- the minor is suffering serious emotional damage, or is at substantial risk of suffering serious emotional damage

- the minor is under the age of five and has suffered severe physical abuse by a parent or guardian, or by any person known by the parent, if the parent knew or reasonably should have known that the person was physically abusing the minor

- the minor's parent or guardian has been convicted of causing the death of another child through abuse or neglect

- the minor has been left without any provision for support

- the minor's parent has been incarcerated or institutionalized and cannot arrange for the care of the minor; or a relative or other adult custodian with whom the child resides or has been left is unwilling or unable to provide care or support for the child, the whereabouts of the parent is unknown, and reasonable efforts to locate the parent have been unsuccessful

- the minor has been freed for adoption from one or both parents for 12 months by either relinquishment or termination of parental rights or an adoption petition has not been granted

- the minor has been subjected to an act or acts of cruelty by the parent or guardian or a member of his or her household, or the parent or guardian has failed to adequately protect the minor from an act or acts of cruelty when the parent or guardian knew or reasonably should have known that the minor was in danger of being subjected to an act or acts of cruelty

According to the W & I Code, it is the intent of the Legislature in enacting this section:

> ...to provide **maximum protection for children** who are currently being physically, sexually, or emotionally abused, being neglected, or being exploited, and to protect children who are at risk of that harm....Nothing in this section is intended to disrupt the family unnecessarily or to intrude inappropriately into

family life, to prohibit the use of reasonable methods of parental discipline, or to prescribe a particular method of parenting.

Abuse includes **acts committed by a parent or caretaker, as well as the failure of the parent or caretaker to protect the child from the acts of others.** These acts are those that endanger the health or safety of a child. In these situations, a child is not able to defend himself or herself and needs some outside authority to step in and provide the necessary protection.

Law Enforcement Authority

The authority of a peace officer to intervene in reported child abuse cases is directly related to the situations described in §300 WIC. The authority itself is derived from the following §305: Any peace officer may, without a warrant, take a minor into **protective custody:**

(a) When the officer has **reasonable cause for believing** that the minor is a person described in Section 300, **and in addition**, that the minor has **an immediate need** for medical care, or the minor is in **immediate danger** of physical or sexual abuse, or the physical environment or the fact that the child is left unattended poses **an immediate threat** to the child's health or safety.

(b) Who is in a hospital and release of the minor to a parent poses an immediate danger to the child's health and safety.

(c) Who is a dependent child of the juvenile court, or concerning whom an order has been made under Section 319, when the officer has **reasonable**

(d) **cause for believing** that the minor has violated an order of the juvenile court or has left any placement ordered by the juvenile court.

(e) Who is found in any street or public place suffering from any sickness or injury which requires care, medical treatment, hospitalization, or other remedial care.

In the typical situation, an officer will be dispatched to **check the welfare** of a child at a home, school, or hospital, or one left unattended in a car parked in a public place. The suspected abuse will have been reported by a neighbor, relative, parent, school official, or private person. That report constitutes **reasonable cause**.

When the officer arrives at the scene, he or she should immediately initiate an investigation to determine if the reported abuse is **founded** or **unfounded**. He or she may take the child into temporary protective custody if it is founded and the situation matches any of the descriptions found in §300 WIC.

Police Discretion and Alternative Dispositions

After completing the investigation, the officer must make a decision as to what action, if any to take. This authority of a police officer is extended to a probation officer or social service worker as well. The officer has four choices, as stated in §307 WIC. The officer may:

- release the minor
- cite the parent or parents of the minor to appear with the minor before the probation officer or social worker
- deliver the minor to the children's shelter or county's dependent housing facility
- take (divert) the minor to a community service program designated for abused or neglected children

In determining which disposition of the minor shall be made, the code states that:

> ... the officer shall give preference to the alternative which **least interferes** with the parents' or guardians' custody of the minor if this alternative is compatible with the **safety of the minor**. The officer shall also consider the needs of the minor for the least restrictive environment and the protective needs of the community.

Notice that the first three alternatives are similar to three of the four choices given a police officer under Section 626 WIC, when handling a 602 juvenile.

At this stage of the proceedings, a dependent child may never be housed or mixed with any 602 juveniles or with any adults in custody. This means that if the officer arrests the parent for the alleged abuse and takes the child into protective custody the parent and child may not ride in the same patrol car. The officer might also need the legally appropriate car seat to transport the child.

In most counties today, children's shelters are administered and staffed by the Department of Social Services. In fact, in most counties, all dealings with §300 cases are now handled by Social Services, including the Intake, court investigations, and aftercare supervision of dependents. The W & I Code refers to the use of probation services throughout the §300 series, but in most cases, probation is no longer involved.

One reason given for this move from probation to social service was the need to facilitate the delivery of services to families by placing them all under one organization. Another, and perhaps more primary reason, was because all funds for probation come from the county budget, whereas a large share of the funds for social service comes from both state and federal sources. By making the move, county governments were able to shift the cost of handling 300 cases to these other levels of government funding.

The alternative choice for a peace officer that was termed *diversion* in §626 is similar to the last alternative an officer has under §307, "...take the minor to a **community service program** for abused or neglected children." The WIC also requires that receiving referrals have a contract or an agreement with the county to provide shelter-care or counseling.

Most counties have such a contract or an agreement, and attempt to ensure that a child is placed in a safe environment in which care, support, and counseling are provided. Social Service will supervise these placements. In addition, many social service departments maintain a network of foster homes where a child or children may be placed temporarily, pending either further investigation, or court action.

The responsibility of a peace officer, probation officer, or social worker who takes a minor into protective custody and delivers him or her to a shelter care facility is specified in §307.4 WIC.

They shall:

...immediately inform, through the most efficient means available, the parent, guardian, or responsible relative, that the minor has been taken into protective custody, and that a written statement is available which explains the parent's or guardian's procedural rights and the preliminary stages of the dependency investigation and hearing.

They shall also explain the conditions under which the minor will be released, that hearings may be required, the means whereby further specific information about the minor's case and conditions of confinement may be obtained, the rights to counsel, privileges against self- incrimination, and rights to appeal possessed by the minor, and his or her parents, guardians, or responsible relative. In addition, a peace officer or social worker must ensure that the following rights of the minor are protected:

- regular telephone contact between the parent and child of any age, unless that contact would be detrimental to the child. The initial telephone contact shall take place...no later than five hours after the child is taken into custody
- no later than one hour after he or she has been taken into custody, a minor 10 years of age or older shall be advised that he or she has the right to make at least two telephone calls from the place where he or she is being held, one call completed to his or her parent, guardian, or a responsible relative, and another call completed to an attorney

Note that any public officer or employee who willfully deprives a minor taken into custody of his or her right to make these telephone calls is guilty of a misdemeanor.

The requirement that an officer shall advise a child over age 10 of the right to make a call to an attorney might seem inconsistent with the nature and purpose of 300 procedures. The child's first reaction, if they understood the advisement at all, might be that he or she is in real trouble. Therefore, the officer will need to clarify the reason for advising the child. There was a time when the officer also had to admonish the child with the *Miranda* warning. This was really inconsistent with the protective nature of 300 WIC.

The Categories of Child Abuse

Three of the four basic categories of child abuse dealt with in this chapter are:

- Physical assault
- Physical neglect
- Emotional maltreatment

Emotional maltreatment is further divided into two sub-categories: emotional assault and emotional deprivation.

Each of these categories is examined below in detail. First, we begin with a legal definition, and then describe the full nature of the category. Next, we look at who abuses their children, and why. Then, we focus on the basic aspects of a police investigation of each category. We conclude the presentation of each type with a summary of the relevant penal code sections an officer would refer to in making an arrest.

Physical Assault

Physical assault is defined **as any act which results in some form of non-accidental physical injury.** The key element of the abuse is "non-accidental" injury. The physical injury most commonly inflicted is by striking, shaking, or throwing a child. However, intentional assaults frequently include burning, biting, cutting, poking, twisting limbs, scalding, or choking a child. These types of injuries fall under Section 300(a) WIC cited above if the parent inflicts them, or 300(b) if the parent fails to protect the child from the actions of others.

The primary target area for inflicting an injury is the back of the child's body from the neck to the knees. These are the areas of the body that are usually covered with clothing, making the injury difficult to see. Or, in the case of burning, parents target the soles of the feet, or palms of the hands. From this, one can conclude that the person inflicting the injury had both the knowledge and intent to do it.

Criminal Law Violations

There are two Penal Code sections to consider when investigating or making an arrest in an abuse situation. Both crimes are what are termed wobblers, chargeable and punishable as either felonies or misdemeanors.

- §273 (d) PC: Inflicting corporal punishment upon a child
- §273 (a) PC: Willful cruelty to children

Who Are the Abusers?

A child can be abused by family, friends, neighbors, acquaintances, teachers, strangers, or childcare providers. However, in a vast majority of the cases the abuser is the parent or friend of the parent; frequently, the mother or the mother's boyfriend. The explanations of why parents abuse are many and varied and cannot be understood within the context of reasonable or unreasonable conduct. Child abuse results from uncontrolled feelings, not rational thoughts. It might result when a parent attempting to administer physical discipline, loses control because of a situational frustration, emotional problems, or excessive fundamentalist religious zeal.

Parenting is no easy task under the best of conditions. Under the stress of emotional, financial, or relationship problems, individuals with dysfunctional parenting skills often vent their frustrations on the one who cannot fight back or who they see as a source of the problem, their child. When a parent mixes discipline with rage, new parenting skills must be learned, and acceptable ways of venting frustration must be found.

Sometimes the parent is remorseful, tries to make amends and promises never to do it again. However, when the frustration reaches that same level, the abusive parent lashes out again, and again, and again. Frequently, this is behavior learned as a child from one's parents. As the biblical expression says: *the sins of the parents shall be visited upon the children even unto the third and fourth generations.* Thus, a **terrible cycle of violence** is created. One learns how to parent by observing and experiencing the behavior from one's own parents.

A person cannot practice what he or she does not possess, and learning positive parenting skills is difficult, at best, from abusive and dysfunctional parents. Re-learning, that is, learning new parenting skills through counseling is quite possible, and is the initial effort taken during early intervention.

Child abuse is the most democratic of all crimes. It is found in families from all social, economic, educational, intellectual, and religious backgrounds. How-ever, more often than not, poverty, social isolation, a lack of access to society's mainstream, fundamentalist religious beliefs, or substance abuse prevails in a home in which abuse occurs. The mother is often the abuser because she is the parent who relates to the child more often, and is under more stress as a parent. The father is either asleep, at work, or absent.

When abuse occurs in a single parent home in which the mother has custody of the child and she has a boyfriend living in the home, the situation might arise in which the boyfriend is the abuser and the mother fails to protect the child. It is not uncommon for a dysfunctional mother to trade off the wellbeing of her child for the presence and/or affection of her boyfriend.

In some cultures that are entering California at an increasing rate, corporal punishment is quite common. It could be considered a direct challenge to parental rights and authority to question their use of physical discipline. These parents need to become acculturated and knowledgeable of our laws, and to clearly understand when police authority will conflict with parental authority. By the same token law enforcement needs to have an appreciation of the parental practices of other cultures. A similar approach is necessary when abuse results from religious zeal.

For example, rubbing a child's body with a coin (coining) is practiced by some Asian cultures. This is not punishment or abuse but merely done for curative purposes.

Police Intervention

Suspected child abuse is reported to law enforcement agencies or county **Child Protective Services (CPS)** from a variety of sources: school officials, doctors, relatives, neighbors, family friends or enemies, clergy, and others.

Frequently, a patrol officer or deputy will be sent to a residence with instructions to *check the welfare* of a child without knowing any details of the situation. The officer's responsibility is to make contact with the child and determine if the health and safety of the child is at risk. As one can see from reading Sections 305 and 307 WIC, the law grants the officer broad authority to fulfill this responsibility and the **welfare of the child takes precedent over the rights of the parent.**

When an officer arrives at a house to check the welfare, he or she should personally inspect the physical condition of all the children and of the house itself. Occasionally, a parent or parents will substitute a healthy child for the one they abuse and hide the abused one. Parents also might object to an officer entering the home and/or will resist the officer's authority. However, since the health and safety of a child or children is at stake, the officer will take whatever reasonable action is necessary to overcome the resistance.

It is usually better to have at least two officers present to enter the house. If abuse is suspected, one officer can inspect and interview the child while the other officer talks to the parent/s in another part of the house. The child will be more willing to talk when the parents are not present. However, the child is placed in a lose-lose position during most any investigation. First, the child often thinks he or she is bad and deserving of the abuse as punishment, so he or she will not tell on parents who are doing the so-called "right thing."

Secondly, if the child does tell on the parent/s, the child might be taken out of the home and from the parents. The child will not want this because, as bad as it is, it is still their home and their parent/s, with who they have bonded in one way or another. Often it is their only source of love and/or attention. Third, if the child is being abused, but does not tell, the abuse will continue. Finally, if the child does tell, but is not taken from the home or parent, he or she runs the risk of being punished by the parent/s for telling.

These are the four worst scenarios but they are not uncommon. Frequently, however, police intervention does result in a positive outcome. A child can be removed from a life-threatening situation; he or she can be placed with a parent or relative who is not abusive and can provide the nurturing a child needs. Or, the parent or parents can learn new parenting skills to establish a functional relationship instead of an abusive one; or one abusive parent or boyfriend can be removed from the scene, allowing the other family members to re-establish their positive relationships.

A second reason for having two officers intervene is for officer safety. One officer alone might need backup, if the decision is made to remove the child because both parents and/or the child or children might resist the officer's actions.

Indicators of Abuse

When physical abuse is suspected, the officers should examine all the children for marks or wounds. Colored photographs should be taken of any wound area, for use in court. The investigating officers also should prepare a pencil sketch that portrays the mark or wound. Colored photographs sometimes are excluded as evidence if they would inflame a jury, but an officer's pencil sketches will almost always be admitted. Even though a photograph is excluded from criminal court proceedings, it usually will be allowed in a juvenile court (civil) hearing.

Bruises are found on the buttocks, back and face. They may appear as an outline of a hand and/or show the impression of an object, such as a ring, coat hanger, ruler, or belt buckle. Linear marks might be left by a belt, electrical cord, or strap. Multiple bruise marks can be all of the same color or of varying shades. Red marks are relatively fresh; black-purple and green tinted ones are about 24 hours old; and pale green or yellow marks reflect a fading to 48 hours or longer. Close-up color photographs should be taken and a ruler and color bar should be included in each photo.

Lacerations reflect a more serious form of abuse than bruises, but they are found in the same areas and portray similar types of weapons. Belts, cords, and buckles often leave a distinct impression. The officer should search the area for any objects that might have been used to inflict the injury. People often grab whatever object is close at hand, and then replace it after administering the discipline. Place any suspected weapons found, carefully, in a plastic bag and identify it for lab analysis.

Bite Marks may be found on any part of the body, and may represent either straight physical abuse or an adjunct to some form of sexual exploitation. They may leave doughnut-shaped, double horseshoe-shaped, or oval shaped impressions of the teeth. Photographs should be taken, with a
measuring device included on each frame. If the bite is fresh and/or deep, salivary swabbing should be taken for analysis of the offender's blood type or DNA composition. A forensic dentist should be called in to collect the swabbing and analyze the bite marks, because this type of evidence, if handled properly can be very useful in identifying the guilty party.

Burns is another common type of punishment. **Scalding** with a hot liquid is the most common form of deliberate burning, and often represents an effort to exorcise evil from the child or to punish the child for fondling himself. Forced burning often leaves clear demarcations, such as when a child is held and has his or her knees or buttocks dipped in hot water. **Immersion** of a hand or foot will leave similar marks. Burning a child with a recognizable object, such as a furnace grill or stove element will leave a telltale mark.

Cigarette burns are usually found on the soles of the feet or palms of the hands, indicating an attempt to conceal the marks. A car lighter burn might be found on the cheek of the child's face, reflecting a temper quick to punish. Burns often go untreated until they become infected. Consequently, immediate medical attention might be necessary.

Head injuries are the most common cause of death from abuse. They can be caused by falling or being thrown, struck, or shaken. Swelling or dark coloration about the head or eyes are obvious signs of injury but such indications are not always present. Damage from the so-called **shaken infant syndrome** might not show up for years or might show early on in the form of learning problems, then show up later in some more serious neurological symptoms.

Blows to the body of a child can cause injuries to other internal organs that might result in death. The obvious physical signs might not be present, but subtle indicators, such as vomiting, blood in the urine, or internal pains are just as significant.

Physical abuse of infants sometimes takes the form of twisting the limbs, hitting, or squeezing the ribs. Fractures are the most common indicator of these types of abuse, and a pattern of fractures of varying ages is strong evidence of abuse.

Police Questioning and Discretion

When questioning parents (or any caretaker) about a child's injury a police officer might encounter one of three explanations:
- the child bruises easily
- he or she fell while playing
- the parent was merely disciplining the child and momentarily lost control

The officer should obtain detailed accounts from the parent/s and the child then ask himself or herself:

> **Does the injury and explanation match the age and activity level of the child?**

It is a good practice to separate the child and parent/s during questioning, and to separate the parents from each other as well. If any of them wants help to stop the abuse he or she will speak more openly to an officer who gives assurance that real help is available.

For all intent and purpose an officer actually has taken custody of the child or children during the home investigation pursuant to §305 WIC. An officer responding to this type of *check the welfare* call has a great deal of discretion and may exercise one or more of the options stated in §307 WIC. In practical terms the provisions of §307 translate into the following options:

> - dismiss the matter and leave the house and child with no follow-up
> - leave the child in the house, but refer the matter to county CPS, or in-house to the detective unit for follow-up
> - take the child to a facility for a medical examination, after which a decision can be made about the continued custody
>
> - cite the parents to bring the child to the probation department or Department of Social Service
>
> - take the child to the county children's shelter, receiving home, or a foster home for protective custody and refer the matter to probation or social service
>
> - take the child to the appropriate community service program
>
> - arrest the parent/s for violating the appropriate Penal Code sections

In deciding which option to take the officer should ask himself or herself several additional questions.

> - Has a crime occurred? If so, what action should be taken against the suspect?

> Will the **IMMEDIATE** health and safety of the child or children be at risk if left in the home?

When physical abuse is evident take the child for a medical examination. It is better to err on the side of the child's safety than to leave the home only to return later with the coroner. A child can always be returned if a medical examination and/or follow-up investigation shows that abuse did not occur.

Physical Neglect

The following definition of neglect is from the Child Abuse and Neglect Reporting Act (which encompasses Penal Code §11164 through §11174.3):

11165.2: As used in this article, "neglect" means the negligent treatment or the maltreatment of a child by a person responsible for the child's welfare under circumstances indicating harm or threatened harm to the child's health or welfare. The term includes both acts and omissions on the part of the responsible person.

> (a) **Severe neglect** means the negligent failure of a person having the care or custody of a child to protect the child from severe malnutrition or medically diagnosed non-organic failure to thrive. "Severe neglect" also means those situations of neglect where any person having the care or custody of a child willfully causes or permits the person or health of the child to be placed in a situation such that his or her person or health is endangered, as proscribed by Section 11165.3, including the intentional failure to provide adequate food, clothing, shelter, or medical care.

> (b) General **neglect** means the negligent failure of a person having the care or custody of a child to provide adequate food, clothing, shelter, medical care, or supervision where no physical injury to the child has occurred.

This category of abuse means that the parent/s have failed to provide a safe and healthy environment for the child. Usually, this is in the form of inadequate clothing, food, shelter, and dental or medical care.

Referrals to police alleging neglect often come from doctors, clinic staff, school officials, relatives, or neighbors concerned about a child's welfare. Such referrals are made after some period of observation by the reporting party, who now expects decisive action in response to his or her report.

The Law Enforcement Investigation

As it was in the case of physical abuse an officer dispatched to a residence to check the welfare in a neglect case should take whatever reasonable action is necessary to enter the house, examine the living conditions and check out all the children as to their health and safety.

There are several key areas that require careful examination. First, check to be sure that the utilities, such as gas, electricity, and water service, are turned on to the house. Next the officer should check the refrigerator to see that it is clean and contains fresh and wholesome food appropriate for the age of the children. Hold the door open and stare at the food for a minute to be certain that none of it moves on its own. Check the cupboards for appropriate food items as well.

Check the sink, counter area, and stove for dirty dishes, and the cupboards for clean ones. It is not uncommon for a parent to use up all the available dishes before washing any or to use dirty and contaminated dishes over again. Also check throughout the house to determine if there is trash, garbage, or animal or human feces about the floor or walls. Check to see if there are any animals in the house, other than pets.

Another important area to check is the room or area where the children sleep. Is the ventilation and heating appropriate for the weather conditions? Is the place (bed) for sleeping clean and adequate? Do the children have adequate clothing? How many children, or people, share the same bed? Is there any odor of urine in the room?

Other areas for inspection include the bathroom. Is it clean? Is the water turned on? If any burn or wear marks were noted around a child's wrists or ankles, check the bathroom plumbing for signs of rope or chain marks. There have been cases where a child has been tied or chained to a shower rod or bathroom plumbing for long periods of time. The bathroom is the logical place for confining a child because of the availability of the toilet and water. Also, one should check all the closets for the odor of urine or feces because **closeting** a child for extended periods of time is a common form of abusive punishment.

Sometimes there is a fine line between physical neglect and sloppy housekeeping. An officer should not impose his or her standards for neatness and cleanliness onto others. There is only one question for consideration: is the child's health and safety at risk, living in the present condition? If not, leave the child in the home. The last thing a court wants to do is separate a child from its natural parent/s. However, a referral to social service might facilitate providing the parent/s with house-keeping skill training. In that case parenting and housekeeping skills will be provided as a part of the supervision.

Emotional Maltreatment

This category of abuse can be divided into two sub-types:

- emotional assault
- emotional deprivation

Both types of emotional abuse are very common, but are the least likely to be referred to police and are the most **difficult to prove**. They can be, nonetheless, devastating to a child.

Emotional Assault

This is any verbal or emotional act that puts the child in danger of suffering emotional trauma. This includes screaming, blaming, sarcasm, belittling, threats, ridicule, criticism, and related acts that are demeaning or emotionally disturbing to a child. It also includes exposing the child to constant family discord, constant negative moods, or unpredictable responses.

Emotional assault of a child or children by parents is usually one of degree, rather than the absolute presence or absence of it. Even the best of parents commits one or more of the acts cited above. Often these are in isolated emotional situations and any harm done is rectified by an apology and/or the expression of positive emotions. When these acts are constant, reflect a pattern, or pervade the parent-child relationship, they are abusive.

Parental rejection or punishment by physical and/or emotional withdrawal is the reverse of assaultive behavior, but it can have the same effects, especially if it is a constant or patterned response.

Consequences of Emotional Assault

Emotional assault frequently contributes to feelings of low self-esteem in the child. These feelings can remain with the abused person for a lifetime. He or she feels unworthy as a person. In later life the abused person might need to confirm these feelings through acts of self-depreciation, and/or by establishing adult relationships which are abusive as well. As it is in the case of most abusive behavior, the child who receives it grows up learning that it is the way to relate. Consequently, he or she may well abuse his or her children. The **terrible cycle** continues.

Indicators of Assault

Emotional assault is difficult to recognize and to prove because it leaves no visible wounds or scars. There are some indicators, however. The child's patterned behavior might be withdrawn, apathetic, clingy, or acting out with verbal aggression, or acting in with acts of self-depreciation. One of the revealing ways to view a child's behavior is to watch him or her play house. Watch how he or she disciplines a doll who is bad and you can get some idea of how that child is treated.

Emotional Deprivation

This is the deprivation suffered by children when their parents do not provide the normal experiences producing feelings of being loved, wanted, secure, and worthy (11164 PC):

From a legal point of view, this definition is rather vague and normative. Perhaps, this is one reason that it is so difficult to prove. This deprivation can occur when parent/s do not express love or warmth, either verbally or physically. Children need to be touched, hugged and told that they are lovable. They need unqualified love. That is, they need to be loved for who they are, not what they do, just like the child in us all. Any consistent pattern to the contrary can create an emotional vacuum in which a child might exist, but may not be able to grow into an emotionally healthy person.

Indicators of Deprivation

Like emotional assault, deprivation **lacks the obvious outward signs** of abuse. Nevertheless, emotional wounds can kill the spirit and numb the senses. They can even create the **failure to thrive syndrome** in which the unloved and untouched child, in effect, curls up and dies.

Many of the symptoms of deprivation are similar to those of emotional assault: **depression, apathy, and withdrawal.** Deprived children might be pesky, but not clingy, because they have not learned how to be close to another person and are fearful of the experience. In fact, they might pull back and avoid any display of affection given them. Also, they may act out in school, or other social settings, and their aggression can reflect a cool and detached attitude.

Consequences of Deprivation

The obvious consequence is that a child grows up feeling unloved and not worthy of love or attention. No one deserves to be deprived of loving and being loved, in a relationship that only parents can provide. Emotional deprivation fosters more of the same. What a person does not know, he or she cannot show. If a person has not learned how to love and be loved when he or she is growing up, he or she will find it difficult to show love to his or her own child. The terrible cycle continues.

One of the most serious consequences of emotional deprivation is the type of person that it can produce. Every serial killer researched by this writer was raised in an **emotional icebox**. Because they were deprived of love for themselves, they have no sensitivity for the feelings of others. In fact, often the only good feeling they derived in relating to others was when they were killing them. For many, they were getting even with the one who denied them love at the start.

Summary

As stated in the introduction this chapter and the one to follow are about a sordid subject, child abuse. This chapter dealt specifically with the physical and emotional abuse of children. They are the most deplorable of all crimes and have an impact on the victim and upon society that is more devastating than any other type of offense. Equally devastating is sexual abuse and exploitation, which is the subject of our final chapter.

Thousands of children are killed every year, and more are beaten and emotionally abused by those who should be providing them with warmth and love. In many instances these abuses are the result of a **cycle of violence** from one generation to the next. It is a cycle that must be broken at any cost.

References

Holm, Marilyn Franzen, *Shall the Circle be Unbroken?: Helping the Emotionally Maltreated Child*.
    Longmont, CO: Bookmakers Guild, 1986.

Wald, Michael. *Protecting Abused and Neglected Children*. Stanford,
    CA: Stanford University Press, 1988.

Internet References

http://www.childabuse.org/
http://child-abuse.com/
http://www.preventchildabuse.org/index.shtml
http://www.safestate.org/index.cfm?navID=6

Chapter 12: Child Sexual Abuse and Dependency Court Proceedings

Key Terms and Concepts

Check the welfare
Child abuse
Child Abuse Reporting Act
Child molestation
Child Protective Services
Clear and convincing evidence
Consequence of abuse
Dependent child
Extra-familial
Foster care

Incestuous
Indicators of abuse
Intra-familial
Lewd acts
Parenting skills
Pedophile
Permanency planning
Pornography
Protective custody
Sexual assault
Sexual exploitation

Introduction

The first portion of this chapter deals exclusively with the sexual abuse and exploitation of children. These acts include a wide array of behaviors, ranging from the abnormal to the very bizarre. The offense might consist of just one act or of many acts over a long period of time. Victims may be of either gender, although the majority are female, and may range in age from a few days to 18 years old. The majority, however, are under 12 years of age.

Reports show that approximately one-third of the victims of sexual abuse are under the age of six years; the vast majority are female; and 96 percent of the offenders are either related to or known by their victims.

We begin with the legal definition of sexual abuse as found in the Penal Code, and note that it is divided into two subsections: (1) sexual assault, and (2) sexual exploitation. Next, we take a cursory look at selected examples of abuse situations, then examine the profile of the typical sex offender. This is followed by an examination of police intervention, indicators of abuse and exploitation, and the consequences of abuse.

The role of Child Protective Services is summarized, then the child abuse reporting laws and sex offender registration laws are detailed.

The final portion of this chapter focuses briefly on juvenile court proceedings that apply in all §300 dependent, neglected, and abused cases.

Sexual Abuse

A lengthy and detailed definition of sexual abuse is provided in the Penal Code, and an array of criminal code sections is contained within the definition. Consequently, the code sections will not be presented separately below. Rather, the complete Penal Code definition is given. First, however, child sexual abuse is placed within the context of §300 WIC so that the reader will continue to keep §300 in mind as the controlling law, and will refer to the appropriate subsection when taking a minor into protective custody under the authority of §305 WIC.

Section 300(d) describes the conditions by which the minor will come within the jurisdiction of the juvenile court when:

> ...the minor has been sexually abused, or there is a substantial risk that the minor will be sexually abused, as defined in Section 11165.1 of the Penal Code, by his or her parent or guardian or a member of his or her household, or the parent or guardian has failed to adequately protect the minor from sexual abuse when the parent or guardian knew or reasonably should have known that the minor was in danger of sexual abuse.

Section 11165.1 of the **Penal Code defines sexual abuse**:

> As used in this article, *sexual abuse* means sexual assault or sexual exploitation as defined by the following:
>
> (a) **Sexual assault** means conduct in violation of one or more of the following sections: 261 (rape), 264.1 (rape in concert), 285 (incest), 286 (sodomy), subdivision (a) or (b) of Section 288 (lewd or lascivious acts
>
> (b) upon a child under 14 years of age), 288a (oral copulation), 289 (penetration of a genital or anal opening by a foreign object), or 647a (child molestation).

(c) Conduct described as "sexual assault" includes, but is not limited to any of the following:

> (1) Any penetration, however slight, of the vagina or anal opening of one person by the penis of another person, whether or not there is the emission of semen.

> (2) Any sexual contact between the genitals or anal opening of one person and the mouth or tongue of another person.

> (3) Any intrusion by one person into the genitals or anal opening of another person, including the use of any object for this purpose, except that, it does not include acts performed for a valid medical purpose.

> (4) The intentional touching of the genitals or groin, inner thighs, and buttocks, or the clothing covering them, of a child, or of the perpetrator by a child, for purposes of sexual arousal or gratification, except that, it does not include acts which may reasonably be construed to be normal caretaker responsibilities; interactions with, or demonstrations of affection for the child; or acts performed for a valid medical purpose.

> (5) The intentional masturbation of the perpetrator's genitals in the presence of a child.

Sexual exploitation is also defined in §11165.1(c) PC and refers to any of the following:

> (1) Conduct involving matter depicting a minor engaged in obscene acts in violation of Section 311.2 (preparing, selling, or distributing obscene matter) or subdivision (a) of Section 311.4 (employment of minor to perform obscene acts).

(2) Any person who knowingly promotes, aids, or assists, employs, uses, persuades, induces, or coerces a child, or any person responsible for a child's welfare, who knowingly permits or encourages a child to engage in, or assist others to engage in, prostitution or a live performance involving obscene sexual conduct, or to either pose or model alone or with others for purposes of preparing a film, photograph, negative, slide, drawing, painting or other

pictorial depiction involving obscene sexual conduct. For the purpose of this section, "persons responsible for a child's welfare" means a parent, guardian, foster parent, or a licensed administrator or employee of a public or private residential home, residential school, or other residential institution.

> (3) Any person who depicts a child in, or who knowingly develops, duplicates, prints or exchanges, any film, photograph, video tape, negative, or slide in which a child is engaged in obscene sexual conduct, except for those activities by law enforcement and prosecution agencies and other persons described in subdivisions (c) and (e) of Section 311.3.

Sexual exploitation would also include:

§266 (j) PC: Providing children for lewd acts.

Any person who intentionally gives, transports, provides, or makes available, or who offers to give, transport, provide, or make available to another person, a child under the age of 16 for the purpose of any lewd or lascivious act as defined in Section 288, or who causes, induces, or persuades a child under the age of 16 to engage in such an act with another person, is guilty of a felony and shall be imprisoned in the state prison for a term of three, six, or eight years, and by a fine not to exceed fifteen thousand dollars.

The Dynamics of Sexual Abuse and Exploitation

For a police investigator, there is no area of human conduct in which one finds such a complete display of what society considers deviant. After a few years of investigating these offenses almost nothing will shock the senses. For example, a man in a northern California county videotaped himself and two others engaged in sexual acts with three young children, including his own. After watching the video, which lasted for over an hour, the prosecutor charged him with 76 separate counts of §288a PC, lewd and lascivious acts against children. Oddly enough, the man pled guilty to all counts and was sentenced to 158 years in state prison.

In a neighboring county, an 18-year-old high school girl confided to her school counselor that her father had molested her several years earlier. The investigation showed that when she reached puberty, about age 14, her father started molesting her.

On occasions, he would leave his own bed where his wife lay sleeping, and enter the bedroom and bed of his daughter. This continued for about two years. It was about then that a younger sister reached puberty. The father stopped molesting the oldest girl and began molesting the younger one. This lasted for about two years, when the youngest girl in the family reached puberty, and the father started with her. The oldest daughter decided to tell on her father because she did not want her younger sister to be subjected to what she and the other sister had gone through.

Investigation also showed that the mother was fully aware of everything, but said nothing. The father pled guilty and was granted probation, with the conditions that he not have contact with the victims and that he participates in counseling. The other family members also attended counseling.

In another case, a single man in his 70s was living in a cottage behind the main house of a family in which lived two young girls. One day he was caught in the parking lot of a local high school attempting to lure a girl into his car with the promise of candy. Investigation showed that in recent years, he had enticed the two girls from the main house, along with six or eight other neighborhood children, into his cottage with the offer of candy and gum. Once inside, he would molest them, but by doing nothing more than touching their genitals or having them touch his.

He never physically harmed, threatened, or scared the girls. The people in the neighborhood, including the children, liked the old man. In fact, the mother of one of the molested girls, who was raised in the neighborhood herself, remembered the occasions when he had enticed her into his cottage and touched her. She never discussed the man with her daughter but she did believe that her daughter probably was being touched, as well. When the story came out most of the neighbors felt sorry for the old man. The court found that he was what is called in legal terms a Mentally Disordered Sex Offender (MDSO), and committed him to Atascadero State Hospital.

In another instance, a couple went to Lake Tahoe with some relatives, to be married. Sometime after the wedding, the groom sexually molested the bride's two-month-old daughter. He worked out a plea-bargain in which he pled no contest to a misdemeanor count and received probation, with jail time as a condition. Also, he was not required to register as a sex offender.

In another case, a man, father of six children, pled guilty to lewd and lascivious conduct with a minor under age 14 years, and was granted probation. In this case, his house was the gathering spot for all the other children in the neighborhood. They all came to play with his children. However, when one particular 13-year-old boy would come, it was understood that his wife would go upstairs and fill the bathtub with water so that her husband and the young boy could bathe together for the next hour or so.

Are these cases weird? Deviant? Abnormal? Are these examples of aberrant behavior? Perhaps they are, but they are not uncommon or unusual. Child abuse is a sordid subject, and sexual abuse and exploitation conjures up the basest of human motivations and behavior.

The Sex Offender

There is no profile of the typical sex offender. They come in all shapes and sizes and are most often either related to or known by the child victim. The vision of the horrible fiend lurking in the shadows and coming out at night to prey upon little children, is a part of the mythology created from those isolated incidents that people fear the most. Incidents that, unfortunately seem to be on the increase. What makes these types of offenses of such concern is the fact that so often the victim is kidnapped at random by a stranger, assaulted, and then killed. In rare instances the child is taken for use in a porn film or a snuff film, a film in which killing the victim is an integral part of the sexual activity.

Aside from these types of crimes, sexual abuse falls into **two categories**: intra-familial and extra-familial abuse. Exploitation is in a category by itself. Each of these is examined in detail below. As the reader will note, the majority of cases involving sexual abuse come from within the home and not from some outside predator.

Intra-familial Abuse

This is the category in which most sexual abuse occurs. It is also the category least discussed and/or displayed in public. **Incest** refers to sexual activity between people who are blood related (§285 PC), and **intra-familial** refers to sexual activities between family members not related by blood.

In most reported cases, the father, stepfather, or substitute father is the offender, with the female child as the victim. However, young boys are also victimized more often than one would think, by either their parents, step parents, or parent substitutes. Older brothers, grandfathers, uncles, male cousins, and boyfriends are offenders as well.

These types of offenses are completed by the persuasion, intimidation or exercise of authority by the adult, and rarely by force. Sometimes the child does not realize what is happening or, if he or she does know, he or she does not know that it is wrong or unusual. Often, however, the act of abuse is followed by threats of harm or promises of gifts, or guilt-provoking pleas for secrecy. Unwanted advances may continue for years because shame, embarrassment, or fear of disgrace can deter a child from reporting the acts.

If he or she wants to report it, to whom does he or she turn for help? In a dysfunctional family a mother might not believe her child and will support the denials of her mate. Sometimes, too, a mother will know about it, but will not intervene to stop it. If she does the man might leave and she will not have a mate on whom she depends emotionally and/or financially. Also, by allowing her mate access to another sexual object, she can avoid fulfilling that role herself.

In some cases, the abused child (usually a female) will realize that if she tells, it will break up her family, and she fears that, or fears being blamed for that. She also might think that an initial advance is an isolated event brought on by some unique situation at hand. Rarely is that the case. Regardless of how casual incestuous or intra-familial abuse begins, it usually increases in demand, frequency, and pressure over the years. Unless the child reports it, she is trapped in a predatory-prey relationship with someone she knows, and may even love, and once trusted.

Extra-familial Abuse

Children who are abused and/or molested by someone outside the family usually know the offender and consider their position with that person to be safe. Although there are several types of sex offenders found in these relationships, the pedophile is the one most frequently encountered.

A **pedophile**, usually a male, views children as his preferred sexual object and his sexual fantasies and erotic images focus on children. He knows that having sex with children is illegal and is a social taboo. However, from his view, it is normal and desirable. It is what gives meaning to his life. Many of them even believe that it is good for the children. Most experts agree that it is next to impossible to change the pedophile. His behavior must either be neutralized or supervised.

Pedophiles often are personable and friendly individuals who get on well with children. They frequently position themselves in a community so as to have maximum access to children. For example, they either volunteer with or assume a professional role in youth clubs, organizations, church activities, or community programs. Consequently, their relationships often are well established with many children in a socially acceptable setting before they initiate any sexual activities. Then they seem to sense the vulnerable or susceptible youth and lure them into a sexual relationship with promises, gifts, or affection. Usually, however, the pedophile spreads his sexual activities among as many children as he can, which makes his offenses increasingly more difficult to conceal. Finally, one of the children tells. Once discovered, it is not uncommon to have many victims be identified (some even going back over many years), making prosecution relatively easy.

Sexual Exploitation and Pornography

The belief is that a substantial number of children are victims of sexual exploitation. However, all the research and documentation available are not able to establish how many. The majority of cases are unofficially undetected and unreported. The problem has become particularly acute since the passage of AB 3121, discussed in Chapter 3. Since then, an increasing number of juveniles have run away within California, and many out-of-state runaways have migrated here, forming a vast pool of unidentified youths waiting to be victimized. To survive the typical runaway must steal or engage in prostitution or pornography.

There are well organized national and international networks of individuals who deal in pornography, some for the profit and others, such as the pedophile, for the sex. Consequently, the photographing and videotaping of children serve a variety of markets for a variety of purposes. They run the gamut from the seemingly innocent nude snapshot to the graphic sexual activity.

The photos or videotapes are either viewed by the pedophile for his own gratification, used to blackmail the victims into silence, used to stimulate other children into participating in similar acts, or sold to other pedophiles or child pornography rings.

Internet chat rooms have been used increasingly by pedophiles to lure young victims into sexual activities. Law enforcement in California and nationwide have seized thousands of films, tapes, computers, and magazines of child pornography. Nevertheless, the exploitation of children seems to thrive unabated.

The problem has been compounded by a recent appellate decision relating to Penal Code sections 311.2 and 311.4. A phrase in those laws states that to be guilty of distributing child pornography, one must know that it depicts a minor engaged in sexual conduct. Consequently, the defense to the charge is merely that one did not know, and had no way of knowing, that any of the people depicted in the magazines or tapes were minors.

Police Intervention

Sexual abuse allegations frequently are referred to law enforcement or child protective services by teachers, school counselors, doctors, parents, relatives, or by the victim. The first rule an officer must follow during the investigation is: **do not believe that what the victim says is true**. In fact, do not necessarily believe what anyone says is true, especially in cases of incestual or intra-familial abuse.

Suspend the need to believe or disbelieve. Simply gather the information, prove and verify what you can, put together the most reasonable explanation possible then decide what action to take. Obviously, this is good police procedure in any investigation. It is mentioned here as a special caution because when a person is accused of child molestation, a stigma attaches to that person that is profound and lasts forever. For example, a police officer friend of this writer was accused of incest by his teenage step daughter. He was suspended from the force pending the investigation, and in the small town where he lived; the entire world knew what he had done. He could not face the humiliation, so he killed himself by gas asphyxiation in his garage. In another local case, a deputy sheriff was accused by his teenage step daughter and two of her friends of molesting them at a slumber party. He faced the music, as it were, pled not guilty, and went to trial.

In both cases, the girls were absolutely and completely lying. In the first case, the girl merely wanted to be accepted and liked by another girl at school, and she thought that confiding such *dark secrets* would make her popular. In the second case, the step daughter wanted revenge against her step father for being too restricting of her social activities. In the first case, the father died. He was a good officer and a good man. In the second case, the charges were dismissed, but the deputy will forever be suspect in the eyes of some people. No actions were taken against the girls who lied.

When called to intervene in a reported case of sexual assault, an officer is called upon to consider a number of factors when considering which disposition to take.

Listed below are those factors most frequently encountered:

- present and future danger to the health and safety of the victim
- need for medical treatment
- victim's need for medical examination
- availability of evidence corroborating the victim's story
- nature and extent of sexual contact
- relationship of victim to suspect
- motivation of victim in reporting offense
- motivation of other parties in reporting offense
- identification of all persons that may have knowledge of the incidents
- descriptions of location/s where act/s occurred
- suspect awareness of the allegations by the victim
- victim's description of any marks, scars, or tattoos on suspect's body
- best approach to use when advising suspect of, and questioning about, the allegations

This list is expanded below to add factors for consideration when investigating a case of sexual exploitation:

- need for a search warrant
- multiple victims and/or suspects
- evidence of nude modeling, performing, or engaging in sexual activities
- evidence of other related child pornography

- victim's description of the acts and where they occurred
- evidence of prostitution
- diaries or journals of suspect or victim
- evidence of sexual activities of suspect on computer discs, films, or videos
- suspect's prior record
- any gifts or rewards received by the victim from the suspect
- suspect's position of trust with the youth
- suspect's formal or informal affiliation with any youth organizations, activities, or programs

These two lists are by no means exhaustive. They should serve as a guide, however, for any preliminary investigation. *

At some point, the officer will need to decide if the minor comes within the description of §300 WIC, and if so, what disposition to make relative to protective custody for the child.

Does the child need the protection of the juvenile court? Or, does the child merely need the suspect removed from the scene? The officer also will need to determine what action to take with the adult offender. In many cases, the minor is taken from the home, either for medical exams or treatment, and the offender is arrested and taken to jail pending criminal prosecution.

In cases of incest or intra-familial sexual abuse, some action should be taken whether to remove the child from the home environment in which sexual abuse is likely to recur, or to remove the offender from the home and deny him access to the victim. In some cases, both actions are necessary. Officer discretion based upon sound professional judgment and the welfare of the child, will dictate which course of action to take.

Indicators of Abuse and Exploitation

There are many indicators of sexual abuse, the presence of which depends upon the type of abuse that has occurred. The more obvious indicators are physical, whereas those that are merely suggestive are behavioral. Below is a list of many of the most common indicators:

- sexually transmitted diseases
- genital discharge or infection
- physical trauma or irritation to the anal/genital areas
- difficulty walking or sitting due to genital pain or trauma
- age-inappropriate knowledge of sexual matters
- inappropriate or aggressive sexual behavior toward peers or toys
- unusual preoccupation with sexual matters or own genitalia
- prostitution or excessive promiscuity
- unusually seductive with others of the opposite sex, usually with adults
- regressive behavior
- school problems or unusual change in school performance
- disturbed sleeping
- withdrawal around adults other than the suspect
- poor hygiene or excessive bathing
- alcohol or drug abuse
- fearful of home, especially if left alone with suspect
- self-destructive behavior
- sudden possession of money or material goods without reasonable explanation for their acquisition*

Consequences of Sexual Abuse and Exploitation

The consequences can be many and varied, depending upon the relationship of the victim to the offender, the gender of the victim, the nature and extent of the abuse or exploitation, and the responses to, and/or labeling of the victim by others.

In a small way, male victims tend to be traumatized less by abuse or exploitation because of the way society (including the victim's parents) views promiscuity by males. More *to-do* is made over a female who has been victimized. She is sometimes perceived by others as having received more trauma, needing more help to get over it, and suffering more *damage* to her own reputation, as it were. In fact, in some cases, it is the reaction to the act that causes the trauma rather than the act itself.

Obviously, serious abuse can cause real and lasting problems for the victim. This is especially true in incestuous or intra-familial acts. These usually are not isolated incidents, but reflect a patterned behavior that extends over some period of time. This can destroy or pervert, forever, the relationships within a family. It can represent one of the most flagrant abuses of trust by a father or step father, or other male family members, and can lead to confusion, hatred and/or blame for one's self and the offender, and create emotional problems that a victim might not ever be able to completely resolve. Also, it often becomes difficult for a victim of molestation to achieve a healthy and functional sexual relationship with an adult of the opposite sex, upon growing up.

A threat to society sometimes results when males are victims of abuse. Many men in prison today for rape, or related aggressive sexual crimes, suffered serious molestation as children. Women who experience serious and repeated sexual abuse might develop a multiple personality. In fact, it is so common that multiple personality is considered symptomatic of child sexual abuse.

Juveniles who run away from home frequently run from parents who are molesting them. For many, however, the only place they can run to is the street where they must prostitution or pornography to survive. Those who run away from so-called normal homes, encounter the same exposure to sexual exploitation. Once they engage in sexual conduct to survive, these youths find it difficult, if not impossible, to ever return to and be accepted by their families.

Child Protective Services

There is an agency of government within each county called the Department of Social Service. Within that organization is a special division known as the Child Welfare Division. That division includes a number of units, each playing a vital role in §300 cases. The **Emergency Response Unit (ERU)**, formerly called Child Protective

Services (**CPS**), provides 24-hour response to reports of child abuse or neglect, including sexual abuse and exploitation. Some name changes are hard to accept and take time to achieve. Such has been the case with Child Protective Services. Consequently, we shall continue the practice of calling it CPS.

Staff from CPS will respond to the scene and investigate the suspected abuse. The Division of Child Welfare only deals with family and household problems, and it does not get involved in any matter that is exclusively criminal. For example, if a child molestation or sexual abuse is suspected at a day care facility, a park, or local school, the investigation is a police matter because the family is not involved. However, if a schoolteacher suspects that child abuse is occurring within the home of a student, it is a matter for both police and CPS.

The police will focus on any criminal violations while CPS will be concerned with the §300 WIC aspects of the case. Police usually will initiate the intervention and CPS will do the §300 follow-up investigation and initiate any action in juvenile court. CPS derives its authority from the following §306 WIC:

> Any social worker in a county welfare department, while acting within the scope of his or her regular duties under the direction of the juvenile court and pursuant to subdivision (b) of Section 272, may do all of the following:
>
> (a) Receive and maintain, pending investigation, temporary custody of a minor who is described in Section 300, and who has been delivered by a peace officer.
>
> (b) Take into temporary custody, without a warrant, a minor who has been declared a dependent child of the juvenile court under Section 300 or who the social worker has reasonable cause to believe is a person described in subdivision (b) or (g) of Section 300, and the social worker has reasonable cause to believe that the minor has an **immediate need** for medical care or is in **immediate danger** of physical or sexual abuse or the physical environment poses an **immediate threat** to the child's health or safety.

Before taking a minor into custody a social worker shall consider whether there are any reasonable services available to the worker which, if provided to the minor's parents, guardian, caretaker, or to the minor, would eliminate the need to remove the minor from the custody of his or her parent, guardian, or caretaker.

Within the Child Welfare Division there exists several other units, each with its own function to perform:

- Court Investigation Unit
- Voluntary Family Maintenance Unit
- Family Reunification Unit
- Permanency Planning Unit

When CPS workers are called to a home, they have discretion as to what action to take. For example, they can refer the family to another agency for counseling. If the family acknowledges that they have a problem and are receptive to intervention, the case may be referred to Voluntary Family Maintenance for a program of training in parenting or homemaking skills. If the child is at risk of sexual abuse and needs to be removed immediately, CPS usually requests law enforcement to take the action. The case is then referred to the Court Investigation Unit to consider court action.

The additional functions and responsibilities of the Child Welfare Division are mentioned, from time to time, below in the presentation on juvenile court dependency proceedings.

Child Abuse Reporting Laws

California is one of the many states having comprehensive reporting laws for suspected child abuse and neglect, including sexual assault and exploitation. They are contained in a series of Penal Code sections from 11164 through 11174.3. The intent and purpose of the law is:

> to protect children from abuse. In any investigation of suspected child abuse, all persons participating in the investigation of the case shall consider the needs of the child victim and shall do whatever is necessary to prevent psychological harm to the child victim.

The law also includes several sections that describe who must report suspected cases of abuse or exploitation.

Those who are legally required to report any and all forms of child abuse include the following:

- all public or private school employees who have contact with or supervision of children
- all employees of public and private youth camps and licensed day care agencies or facilities
- employees of any child protective agency
- all health care practitioners
- all commercial film and photographic print processors

The specific nature of the reporting procedures and report forms also are described within the above-cited sections. Under Penal Code Section 11172, anyone required to report suspected abuse and neglect has **no civil or criminal liability** as a result, regardless of whether the abuse is unfounded or unsubstantiated after an investigation.

Sex Offender Registration

Anyone convicted of the commission or attempt of the sex offenses listed above under the category of sex abuse is required under Penal Code Section 290 to register with the local law enforcement agency having jurisdiction where the offender lives. Juvenile §602 wards committed to CYA for the commission or attempt of these sex offenses also must comply with the registration procedures. This registration law is designed to control all convicted sex offenders, not just those who victimize children.

Section 290 is long and complex and is written to cover all circumstances related to sentencing for a conviction of almost every type of sex offense. Every person convicted must register with the appropriate agency within 14 days of residing in that agency's jurisdiction. This means that if convicted and released into the community on probation, released from jail, prison, or a mental hospital, the offender must register.

Each convicted offender is informed of this requirement before release and must sign a form acknowledging that he or she understands the law. The form contains the offender's intended address upon release and is sent to the State Department of Justice

(DOJ) for the purpose of tracking the offenders. The appropriate law enforcement agency is notified of the offender's pending release and address.

If a sex offender relocates, he or she must not only register with the law enforcement agency in the new jurisdiction, he or she must notify the present agency of the move and new address. DOJ is also notified of each new registered address. Anyone convicted of failing to register is guilty of a felony, punishable by either sixteen months, two years, or three years in prison. Also, any person on probation or parole who fails to register shall have his or her probation or parole revoked.

Anyone required to register shall, at the time of release into the community, be required to provide two samples of blood and a saliva sample for DNA analysis by DOJ.

Any 602-juvenile required to register will be relieved of this requirement on reaching age 25. However, any adult required to register for a misdemeanor conviction, may not be relieved of this by having the conviction expunged (a legal procedure detailed in Penal Code §1203.4 to reverse the conviction and dismiss the charges). Any adult convicted of a felony is required to register for the rest of his or her life, unless granted a Certificate of Rehabilitation pursuant to Penal Code Section 4852.01.

Anyone may call the Child Molester Identification Line, 900-463-0400 to inquire if a specific person they identify is a registered sex offender. There is a fee for this call. Residents also may go to their local law enforcement agency and view, on a CD, a list of registered sex offenders living within their postal code.

Juvenile Court Dependency Proceedings

All dependency proceedings come within the **exclusive jurisdiction** of the juvenile court. This jurisdiction may be exercised by the county within which the alleged abuse occurred, in which the minor was taken into protective custody, or in which the minor resides. The purpose of juvenile court law in dependency cases is defined as follows:

> to provide maximum protection for children who are currently being physically, sexually, or emotionally abused, being neglected, or being exploited, and to protect children who are at risk of that harm.

The procedures by which a dependent child is processed through the juvenile court are very similar to those procedures used when dealing with 602 delinquents. The purpose of the proceedings, some of the vocabulary used, and a few of the responsibilities of the court personnel differ, but the basic process is the same. Consequently, the court proceedings are not presented in great detail here.

Basis for Dependency

Procedures begin when a CPS worker or police officer investigates a report of suspected abuse or neglect, and decides that the report is substantiated and that the child comes within the description of Section 300 WIC. When the officer either cites the parents or delivers the minor to probation or social services pursuant to Section 307 WIC, the child is initiated into the process. Thereafter, the discretion of either a hearing officer, or an Intake Officer or social worker, within one of those agencies, decides if further action is necessary.

The district attorney will decide whether to prosecute any adult offender in criminal court if one is arrested, but will have no say if the child-victim is to be referred to juvenile court. That decision can be made only by a probation officer or social service intake worker. As indicated earlier in this chapter, the responsibility in most counties lies with the Department of Social Service.

The Role of Intake

The Intake Officer reviews the investigative reports and decides how the case should proceed. Intake may dismiss the matter if he or she believes that the investigative facts fail to substantiate the alleged abuse. If Intake believes that the minor is, or soon will be, within the jurisdiction of the juvenile court, he or she may initiate a program of informal supervision that attempts to remove or change the conditions that brought the minor within the description of §300 WIC. The parent/s must agree to participate in this program for Intake to use it. If Intake believes that court action is necessary, he or she may file a petition with the court to have the minor declared a dependent of the court.

Regardless of what action Intake decides is necessary, the minor must be released to the custody of his or her parent/s, guardian, or responsible relative unless one or more of the following conditions exist:

- the minor has no parent, guardian, or responsible relative; or the minor's parent, guardian, or relative is not willing to provide care for the minor

- continued detention of the minor is a matter of **immediate** and **urgent** necessity for the protection of the minor and there are no reasonable means by which the minor can be protected in his or her home or the home of a responsible relative

- there is substantial evidence that a parent, guardian, or custodian of the minor is likely to flee the jurisdiction of the court

- the minor has left a placement in which he or she was placed by the juvenile court

The Petition

If Intake believes that court action is necessary, he or she will file a petition to commence proceedings in juvenile court. It shall include the names and addresses of all the parties relevant to the action, whether the minor is detained pending court, and a concise statement as to the facts that bring the minor within the description of Section 300 WIC.

The petition must be filed within 48 hours (excluding non-judicial days) of the minor being taken into custody. If the minor is detained for longer than six hours and a petition is not filed, Intake must provide the parent/s with a written explanation as to why custody was necessary.

When a petition is filed, the clerk of the court shall set the matter for a hearing within 15 days, if the minor is detained, or within 30 days if not detained. The parent/s or guardian shall be sent a copy of the petition and a notice of hearing as soon as possible, or at least within five days, if the minor is detained, and ten days if not. The notice shall also advise the parent/s or guardian that all parties to the action have a right to be represented by counsel, and that one may be appointed if any of the parties cannot afford one.

The Detention Hearing

If the minor is detained pending court, the court must conduct a detention hearing as soon as possible but in any event by the next judicial day after the petition is filed.

At their appearance in court, all parties will be advised of the reason the minor was taken into protective custody, the nature of the juvenile court proceedings, and the rights of each to be rep-resented by counsel. The court will appoint counsel for the minor whenever it appears that the minor can benefit from representation. Usually this happens in every case. Usually, the district attorney is the one appointed to represent the minor.

The Adjudication/Jurisdictional Hearing

This is a fact-finding hearing to determine if the allegations in the petition are true, just as it was in the 602 proceedings described in Chapter 8. However, in 300 cases, this hearing is not as formal, nor as adversarial as it would be in 602 cases, unless the matter is contested. The testimony of a minor may be taken in chambers and outside the presence of the minor's parent or parents. If the minor's parent or parents are represented by counsel, the counsel may be present in chambers if any of the following circumstances exist:

➢ the minor is likely to be intimidated by a formal courtroom setting

➢ the minor is afraid to testify in front of his or her parent or parents

➢ the court determines that testimony in chambers is necessary to ensure truthful testimony

If the allegations are contested, the proceedings might become adversarial because the district attorney must present witnesses and other evidence to prove the facts. The defense attorney representing the parents may cross-examine and present evidence to counter the allegations.

At the adjudication/jurisdictional hearing, the court shall first consider only the question of whether the minor is a person described by §300. For this purpose, any matter or information and material relevant to the circumstances or acts which are alleged to bring him or her within the jurisdiction of the juvenile court is admissible and may be received in evidence. Proof by a **preponderance of evidence**, legally admissible in the trial of civil cases, must be used to support a finding that the minor is a person described by §300.

The Dispositional Hearing

After a finding that the allegation is true, the court will hear any and all evidence as to the proper disposition in the case. The court may and usually does continue the matter for up to 10 days for a dispositional hearing if the minor is detained, or up to 30 days if not detained. The court will refer the case to either probation or social service for an investigation and written report detailing the offense and the social and personal history of the parents and the minor. The report will include a recommendation as to the appropriate disposition. Copies of this report will be provided to the court, parent/s or guardian, and counsels.

The last order the court wants to make is the removal of any child from the care and control of his or her parent/s. As Justice Baxter stated in the decision ***In re* Kieshia, 1993**:

> Because we so abhor the involuntary separation of parent and child, the state may disturb an existing parent-child relationship only for strong reasons and subject to careful procedures.

Every effort will be made to change or remove the conditions that caused the child to come within the description of Section 300 before out-of-home placement is ordered. The court may implement a period of informal supervision by probation or social service to change those conditions and provide whatever services are necessary to the family (also see, ***In re* Jasmine G., 2000**).

If that disposition proves ineffective, or is not warranted, the court may declare the child to be a dependent of the court. At that point, the court sits in *loco parentis*, and the following WIC procedures apply:

> ➤ §361(a) In all cases in which a minor is adjudged a dependent child of the court on the grounds that the minor is a person described by Section 300, the court may limit the control to be exercised over the dependent child by any parent or guardian and shall by its order clearly and specifically set forth all such limitations. Any limitations on the right of the parent or guardian to make educational decisions for the child shall be specifically addressed in the court order. The limitations shall not exceed those necessary to protect the child.

- §362(a) When a minor is adjudged a dependent child of the court on the grounds that the minor is a person described by Section 300, the court may make any and all reasonable orders for the care, supervision, custody, conduct, maintenance, and support of the minor, including medical treatment, subject to further order of the court.

The W & I Code contains complex descriptions of the situations in which a child may be taken from his or her parent. In essence, no dependent child shall be taken from the physical custody of his or her parent/s or guardian with whom the child resides at the time the petition is initiated unless the juvenile court finds **clear and convincing evidence (*In re* Isayah C.,2004)** of any of the following:

- there is a substantial danger to the physical or emotional health of the minor or would be if the minor was returned home

- the parent or guardian of the minor is unwilling to have physical custody of the minor

- the minor or a sibling of the minor has been sexually abused, or is deemed to be at substantial risk of being sexually abused

If the court orders a child removed from the custody of a parent it will give preference to placing the child with another parent, or with a responsible relative. If one is not available or appropriate, the court can place the child in a foster home or home care facility. The court also can order any parental visitation arrangement that is appropriate for the welfare of the minor.

Any out-of-home placement will be reviewed every six months, with the thought of returning custody to the parent/s. And, at any such hearing, the custody of the child will be returned to the parent/s unless, by a preponderance of evidence, the court finds "…that return of the child would create a substantial risk of detriment to the physical or emotional well-being of the minor."

During any period of out-of-home placement, the minor is supervised by probation or social service, and every effort is made to change the conditions that caused dependency, and to reunite the child with his or her parents. If it appears to the court that the minor cannot be returned home because of the substantial risk, it will schedule a permanency planning hearing within 12 to 18 months of the out-of-home placement order. At that time, the court will determine the probability of the minor being returned home within the next six months.

If it appears that the minor cannot be returned to the custody of his or her parents the court will develop a permanent plan for the minor. It will authorize the appropriate agency to proceed to free the minor completely from the legal custody of his or her parents and initiate adoption plans unless any of the following three conditions exist:

- the parents or guardians have maintained regular visitation and contact with the minor and the minor would benefit from continuing this relationship

- a minor 10 years of age or older objects to the termination of parental rights

- the minor's foster parents, including relative caretakers, are unable to adopt the minor

The 4th DCA held that before a juvenile court can terminate parental rights and prepare a case for adoption, it must find by **clear and convincing evidence**, that returning the child home poses a substantial risk to the child, and that the child will likely be adopted. This is a standard higher than a mere preponderance of the evidence. (***In re* Cassandra V., 1992, *In re* Anita G., 1993**)

Within the context of that standard, the court will make every effort to establish a permanent and stable home for a dependent child in accordance with the legislative intent as expressed below.

Summary

This chapter began with the legal definition of sexual abuse as found in the Penal Code and divided abuse into sexual assault and sexual exploitation. We took a cursory look at selected examples of abuse situations, then examined the profile of the typical sex offender. This was followed by an examination of police intervention, indicators of abuse and exploitation, and the consequences of abuse.

The role of Child Protective Services was summarized, then the child abuse reporting laws and sex offender registration laws were detailed. The final portion of this chapter focused on juvenile court proceedings that apply in all §300 dependent, neglected, and abused cases.

The protection of abused and neglected children is the most fundamental responsibility of the juvenile court. Here, the protective pillars of the system, *parens patriae* and *loco parentis*, must stand firm. The timely and effective intervention by police officers and CPS workers must continue providing the strong support children need.

Abuse is a sordid subject, but one which demands our immediate attention. We need a comprehensive plan to make substantial resources available to combat the crimes against the most vulnerable among us, our children. It should follow that any reduction in child abuse will have a resounding ripple effect. It should reduce crime substantially. For all of our sakes, we must stop the **terrible cycle of violence.**

References

Comte, Jon R. *A Look at Child Sexual Abuse*. Chicago: National Committee for the Prevention of Child Abuse, 1986.

Holm, Marilyn Franzen, *Shall the Circle be Unbroken?: Helping the Emotionally Maltreated Child*. Longmont, CO: Bookmakers Guild, 1986.

Snyder, Howard N. and Melissa Sickmund. *Juvenile Offenders and Victims: 1999 National Report*. Pittsburgh, PA: National Center for Juvenile Justice, 1999.

Wald, Michael. *Protecting Abused and Neglected Children*. Stanford, CA: Stanford University Press, 1988.

Internet References

http://www.acf.hhs.gov/programs/cb/pubs/cm04/summary.htm

http://www.ncptsd.va.gov/facts/specific/fs_child_sexual_abuse.html

http://myspace.com/childabuse

http://caag.state.ca.us/childabuse/forms.htm

http://www.safehorizon.org/page.php?nav=sb&page=childabuseincest

http://www.capcsac.org/childabuse/laws.html

Case Decisions

In re Anita G. (1993) 14 CA 4th 549

In re Cassandra V. (1992) 10 CA 4th 3150

In re Isayah C., (2004) No. J0426742 CA 5th

In re Jasmine G. (2000) No. G026130 CA 4th

In re Kieshia (1993) 6 CA 4th 68

Case Citations

A

Alejandro N. v. Superior Court, 2015…153

Alfredo A. v. Spr. Crt, 1993…..104

B

Baldwin v. Lewis, 1969….98
Breed v. Jones, 1975…..82

E

Ex Parte Ah Peen, 1876…..8
Ex Parte Crouse, 1838…..6

F

Fare v. Michael C., 1979….54, 56
Florida v. Royer, 1983…..38

G

Gagnon v. Scarpelli, 1973…..139
Gonzales v. Mailliard, 1971…..17
Guillory v. CA, 2003…..82

I

In re Ah Peen, 1876…..8
In re Alejandro N. v. Superior Court, 2015..131
In re Aline D., 1975…..148
In re Anita G., 1992…..198
In re Anthony J., 1980…..62
In re Antonio, C., 2000…..133
In re Bonnie H., 1997…..54
In re Bryant R., 2003…..148
In re Cassandra V., 1992…..198
In re Daniel D., 1995…..31
In re Donaldson, 1967…..64
In re Eugene R., 1980…..148
In re Francis W., 1974…..139
In re Frankie J., 1988…..132

In re Gary Steven J., 1971…..82
In re Gault, 1967…..54, 79
In re Gerald B., 1980…..133
In re Glen J., 1979…..139
In re Glenn R., 1970…..39
In re Humberto, 2000…..30
In re Isayah C., 2004….197
In re Jaime P., 2006….66
In re James Edw. D., 1987….30
In re James S., 1978…..138
In re Jasmine G., 2000…..196
In re J. L. P., 1972…..116
In re Josh W., 1997….133
In re Kenny A., 2000…..120
In re Kieshia, 1993…..196
In re Kirk G., 1977…..120
In re Lawanda L., 1986…..148
In re Manuel L., 1993…..98
In re Maria A., 1975…..120
In re Martin L., 1986…..138
In re Melvin J., 2000…124
In re Michael G., 1988…..29
In re Michael T., 1993….111
In re Nancy C., 1972…..33
In re Ricky H., 1981….148
In re Robert M., 1985…..134
In re Roger S., 1977…..83
In re Scott K., 1979…..82
In re Sheena K., 2007…..133
In re Steven C., 1970….82
In re Todd L., 1981…..132
In re Tony C., 1978…..39
In re Tyrell J., 1994…..65, 132
In re Winship, 1970…..80

J

J.D.B. v. North Carolina, 2011…55

Case Citations

K

Kent v. U. S., 1966.....77

M

Mailliard v. Gonzales, 1974.....18
Mapp v. Ohio, 1961.....61
McKeiver v. Pennsylvania, 1971.....81
Miranda v. Arizona, 1966.....53

N

New Jersey v. Lowry, 1967.....61
New Jersey v. T.L.O., 1985.....63

P

Pennsylvania Board of Probation and Parole v. Scott, 1998.....62
People v. Burton, 1971.....56
People v. Delvalle, 1994.....133
People v. Ingham, 1992.....31
People v. Jimenez, 1978.....56
People v. Lara, 1967.....56
People v. Maestas, 1987.....56
People v. McLaughlin, 1991...104
Peoples v. Robinson, 1986.....133
People v. Sanders, 2003.....67
People v. Walton, 1945.....32
People v. Westbrook, 2002.....121

S

Safford Unified School Dist, et.al., 2009 63
Schall v. Martin, 1984.....105
State (New Jersey) v. Lowry, 1967....61

T

Terry v. Ohio, 1968.....39

U

U. S. v. Juvenile Male, 2000....*112*
U. S. v. Mendenhall, 1980.....39
U. S. v. Rudolfo R., 2000.....58

W

Weeks v. U. S., 1914.....60

Y

Yarborough v. Alvarado, 2004....54

Juvenile Procedures in California - 8th edition

Subject Index

A

Adjudication Hearing
    Delinquency.....109
    Dependency.....195
Age of Responsibility.....1, 184
Allegations.....100, 110
Assembly Bill 3121....24
At risk youth.....25
At Risk Early Intervention
    Programs.....29
Augustus, John.....7

B

Beyond control.....22
Borstel system.....6

C

California Youth Authority...16
    History of.....143
    also see
      Division of Juvenile
        Facilities...142
Chancery Court.....3
Child Abuse
    categories of.....164
    indicators of.....167
Child abuse reporting law.....190
Child Protective Services....165, 188
Citation hearing.....123
Cloceting.....172
Common law heritage..... 2
Confinement time.....142
Consensual encounter
    by police.....38
Consent search.....38
Courtesy supervision.....136
Curfew procedures.....31

Custodial interrogation.....53
Cycle of violence.....164

D

Defense strategies.....111
Deferred entry of
    judgment.....122
Deinstitutionalization.....20
Delinquency.....37
Delinquent....37
Dependency proceedings.....192
Dependent child 157
Detention by police.....39
Detention criteria,
    in juvenile hall.....105
Detention hearing
    for delinquent cases.....104
    for dependent cases.....194
Direct filing procedures...84, 93
Discretion for police.....43, 164
Dispositional hearing.....113, 116, 196
District Attorney
    role in delinquent cases....102
    role in dependent cases....195
Division of Juvenile
    Facilities....120, 142
    parole board.....146
    parole consideration.....151
    population profile.....145
Dixon Bill (AB 3121)....22

E

Emotional assault.....172
Emotional deprivation.....173
Emotional maltreatment.....1172
Exclusionary Rule.....68

Subject Index

Extra-familial sexual abuse.....182

F
Failure to thrive syndrome.....174
Fifth Amendment
    admonishment by police.....52
Finding of fact, by judge.....91, 112
Finding of fitness.....91
Fitness criteria.....91
Fitness hearing....77, 90
Fourth Amendment.....60
    also, see Police searches of
    probationers and parolees
Fricot School for Boys.....17
Functional specialization
    in law enforcement.....36
    in probation......127

G
Gang enhancements.....70
Gang formation & activities....68
Gang offenses.....70
Gang registration.....69
Gang suppression.....72
Gang Violence and Juvenile
    Crime Prevention Act.....43

H
Home supervision.....91, 108
House of Refuge..... 7

I
Illinois Juvenile Court Law.....7
Incestuous abuse.....181
Incorrigible.....24
Independent State Grounds.....54
Infield showup.....40
Informal probation.....101. 117

Intake Probation Officer....15,100,193
Interested adult laws.....58
Interstate Compact
    Agreement.....136
Intrafamilial sexual abuse.....181

J
Jamestown, training ship.....9
Jeopardy.....83
Judicial waiver.....90
Jumping-in, a gang.....68
Jurisdictional hearing....109
Jurisdiction waiver
    procedures.....83
Justice Model.....128
Juvenile Justice and Delinquency
    Prevention Act of 1974.....19
Juvenile
    Chancery Court.....4
    court law of 1903.....9
    court law of 1915.....11
    court law of 1961.....12
    court law of 1976.....22
    purpose of.....114
    custody by police.....37
    custody in law enforcement
        facility.....36
Juvenile Hall.... 105
Juvenile Re-entry Grants....134

K
King's Chamberlain's Court.....3

L
Labeling theory.....19
Law Enforcement
    authority to intervene
        in delinquent cases.....40

Juvenile Procedures in California - 8th edition

Subject Index

      in dependent cases.....159
Legislative waiver.....84
Loco Parentis.....8
Los Guilicos School.....13, 112

M
Magdelen Asylum.....9
Medical Model.....19
Miranda warning.....53
      also see, Fifth & Sixth
          Amendments
Miranda warning in Federal
               cases.....58
Missing Persons
            Procedures.....26

N
Neglect....170

P
Parens Patriae..8, 15, 80, 156
Parole searches....66
Parole Board.....146, 151
Pedophile.....186
Petition.....3, 7, 15, 96, 102, 194
Physical abuse.....163
Physical assault.....163
Physical neglect.....170
Police, see Law Enforcement
Poor laws.....4
Preponderance of evidence.....7, 80
Prima facie case.....107
Probation
    authority of officer.....128
    caseload assignment
           models.....131
    conditions of.....13
  Intake officer.....97, 128

    organization of.....126
        reports.....115
        supervision.....129
        searches.....64
    violation and revocation
          procedures.....138

R
Re-entry dispositional hearing...134
Record sealing.....137
Rehabilitation Model.....115
Reform School system.....9
Runaways.....23

S
San Francisco Industrial
    School.....9
San Quentin (used for
    juveniles).....9
School searches.....61
Sealing of records.....137
Search of truants.....30
Secure custody in a law enforce-
    ment facility.....46
Senate Bill 1391.....84
Sexual abuse.....147
Sexual assault.....177
Sexual exploitation.....178, 183
Sex offender.....181
Sex offender registration
              law.....191
State Reform School of
    Marysville.....9
Status offender.....1, 14
Status offense.....1, 14
STEP Act.....70
Street gangs.....70
Supplemental petition....138

T

Task force…..73
Terrible cycle of violence…..164
Totality of the Circumstances, standard….32
Transfer (of court jurisdiction) hearing..92
Truancy…..24, 28

V

Ventura School for Girls…..9
Void-for-vagueness doctrine…17, 32, v118

Ward…..118
Wardship…..118
   termination of…..136
Welfare and Institutions Code,
  Sections: 602…37
          601…..22
          300…..156
          707….84
          625….56
Whittier School for Boys…..9

Y

Youth Authority, see Division of Juvenile Facilities…..143
Youth Parole Board…..146

Made in the USA
San Bernardino, CA
31 January 2019